Yoko's Diary

Yoko's Diary

The life of a young girl in Hiroshima during WWII

Edited by
Paul Ham

Translated by
Debbie Edwards

ABC
BOOKS

The ABC 'Wave' device is a trademark of the Australian Broadcasting Corporation and is used under licence by HarperCollins*Publishers* Australia.

HarperCollins*Publishers*
Australia • Brazil • Canada • France • Germany • Holland • India
Italy • Japan • Mexico • New Zealand • Poland • Spain • Sweden
Switzerland • United Kingdom • United States of America

HarperCollins acknowledges the Traditional Custodians of the lands upon which we live and work, and pays respect to Elders past and present.

First published in Australia in 2013
This edition published on Gadigal Country in 2025
by HarperCollins*Children'sBooks*
a division of HarperCollins*Publishers* Australia Pty Limited
ABN 36 009 913 517
harpercollins.com.au

HarperCollins*Publishers*
Macken House, 39/40 Mayor Street Upper
Dublin 1, D01 C9W8, Ireland

A catalogue record for this book is available from the National Library of Australia.

ISBN 978 0 7333 4409 1

Cover and internal design by Matt Stanton, HarperCollins Design Studio
Cover images: Yoko Moriwaki (front) and Yoko with other shine maidens (back) supplied by Kohji Hosokawa; all other images by shutterstock.com
Typeset in Sabon by Kirby Jones
Printed and bound in Australia by McPherson's Printing Group

MIX
Paper from responsible sources
FSC® C001695

Contents

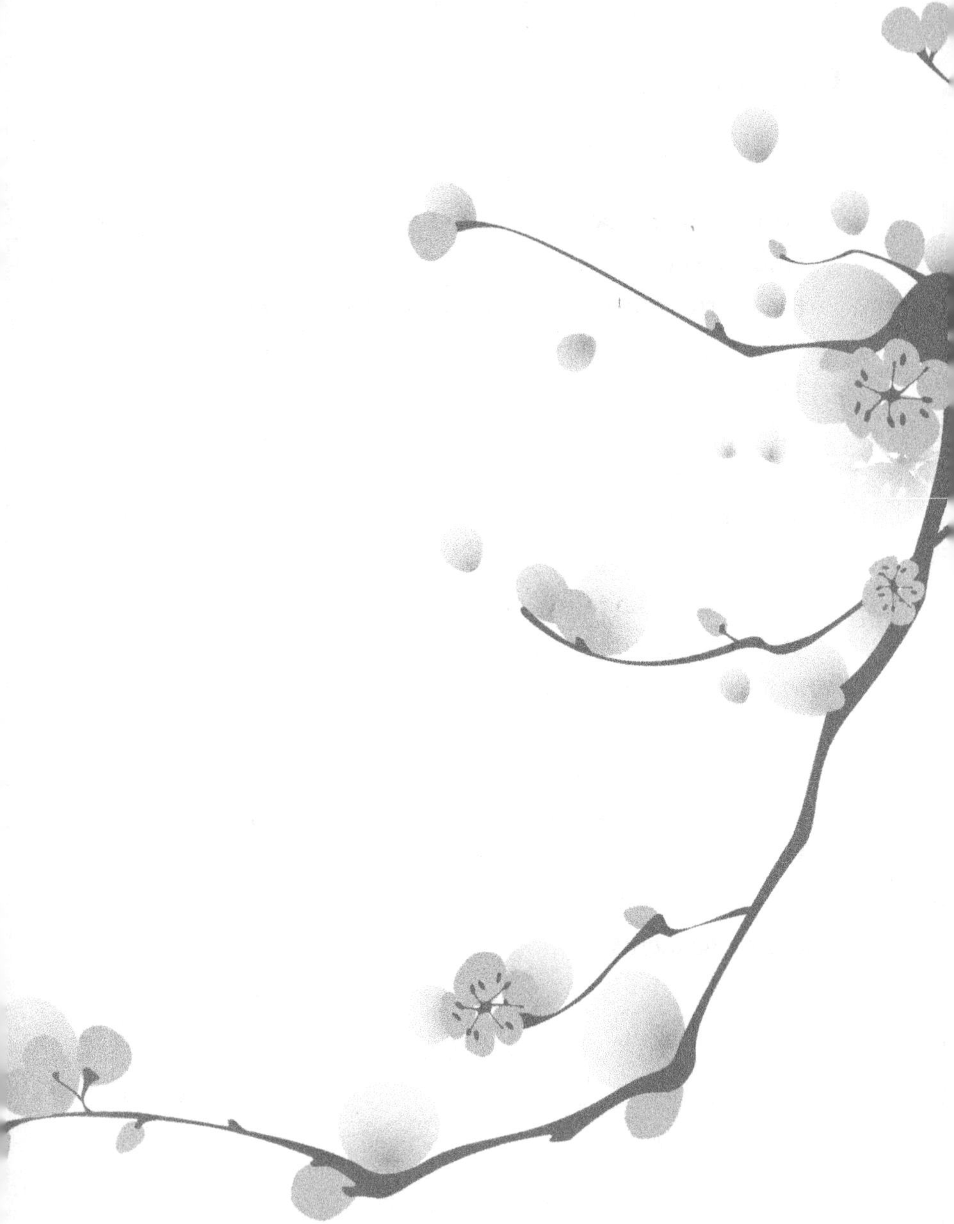

A girl in Hiroshima

Finding Yoko

by Paul Ham

She was just like you or any other twelve-year-old child who got up every morning and went to school. She loved her mum and dad. She laughed at some of her teachers. She worked hard. She enjoyed school and her friends and holidays. But Yoko Moriwaki was unlike you in that she lived in Japan, not far from the southern Japanese city of Hiroshima, during the worst war the world has ever known.

This edition of *Yoko's Diary* is being published to commemorate the eightieth anniversary year of the dropping of the atomic bombs on Hiroshima and Nagasaki, which killed 100,000 civilians instantly, and many hundreds of thousands more, in later years, from bomb-related cancers. Yoko was among thousands of schoolchildren, many as young as eight, who bore the full impact of the Hiroshima bomb.

Yoko and her family lived on the lovely mountainous island of Miyajima, home to one of the most beautiful religious shrines in Japan. They shared a small house made of traditional Japanese paper. Her father was a music teacher.

Until 1941, when the war broke out, her life was fairly typical of most Japanese girls. She went to school, learned the piano, was cared for by her family, she performed her ceremonial duties. She was taught to believe in a religion called Shinto, the ancient Japanese faith. At the heart of Shinto in the mid-twentieth century was a belief in, and worship of, the Emperor as a living god.

When the war came, Yoko's life changed completely. Slowly the towns began to lose their young men, as brothers and fathers left to fight in the Pacific. In 1944 Yoko's father was called up. As Japan began to lose the war, food started running out, and by 1945 even rice, the Japanese staple diet, grew scarce. She and her family ate sweet potatoes and berries and anything they could find in the forests.

Her school uniform changed too. Japanese girls loved their sailor-suit uniforms, but due to wartime austerity, junior students had to go without them. In some places the authorities believed the white uniforms made children visible to enemy planes, and banned them. Instead girls had to make their own uniforms. Many happily sewed their own clothes, often during class time. Yoko's mother found an old kimono, took it apart and sewed it into a small dress for Yoko. As the war worsened and Yoko and her classmates were mobilised to work as labourers, she was compelled to wear the drab grey trousers and shirt called *monpe*.

Towards the end of the war, Yoko worked as a student labourer on one of the house demolition sites. She was one of about 7500 student workers in Hiroshima aged between twelve and eighteen. One of her jobs was to clear debris from demolished homes to create firebreaks and thus prevent fires from spreading after a bombing attack. By mid-1945 most big

Japanese cities had been heavily bombed and reduced to ashes. The people of Hiroshima were warned to expect the same. But as late as July 1945, Hiroshima and four other Japanese cities remained eerily untouched. In fact the American forces had set them aside as targets for the atomic bomb.

On the night of 5 August, Yoko prepared for another day as a mobilised student worker: 'From tomorrow morning we are joining the home demolition groups. I am going to do my best,' she wrote.

The next morning she got up early, travelled to the city, reached the demolition site, took off her dress, and put on her *monpe*. At 8.15am a plane flew overhead. A large object fell out. It was the first atomic bomb ever to be dropped on human life. Suddenly there was a great flash and the temperature shot up to many times that of the surface of the sun. Then a tremendous shockwave convulsed the city and blew apart most of the buildings. Anyone standing within a 2-kilometre radius of the blast was horribly burned or struck by flying debris. Yoko stood 700 metres away, in the open air, without any protection. Her little body was blown into the air and dreadfully burned. But astonishingly, she survived the immediate blow. She began crawling on her hands and knees to a place of safety. An army truck picked her up and drove her out of the city centre. A volunteer housewife found her near lifeless body in a village school that was doubling as a relief centre near Hiroshima, and tried to ease her agony.

I came across the story of Yoko while researching my book on the atomic bomb, *Hiroshima Nagasaki*. In 2010, I stayed in Hiroshima and met Yoko's half-brother, Kohji Hosokawa, then in his eighties (Yoko and Kohji had the same mother, but different fathers). I recall him holding up Yoko's handwritten notebook. 'This is her diary,' he told me, his voice still shaking at the memory of his little sister. 'You can see that it begins from the day she entered school ... and how happy and proud she is to become a student.'

Yoko's brother, Kohji, showed me the pen Yoko used to write her diary. It has an old-fashioned nib, which she would dip into an inkpot. He pointed to a black trace and said, 'The ink remaining on the pen is the ink she was using on 5 August. I don't touch that part of the pen.' And he showed me photos: of a little girl sitting at the piano; of the same girl in a pretty dress wearing a hat.

In 1996 Kohji published Yoko's diary in Japan. He had been encouraged to do so by a teacher from Hosei University Girls' High School, Hiroshi Kamei, who for many years had been bringing students from Yokohama, across the Japanese island of Honshu, to Yoko's old high school, on a field trip to the location of the world's first atomic bombing. Yoko's diary was one of the objects his students examined, and Kamei encouraged Kohji to publish it as a record of the time, which would be available to everyone in Japan. The diary had already been used poignantly in a documentary, *Girls in Summer Dresses – Hiroshima – 6 August 1945*. As you will read in his introduction, Kohji decided he would indeed publish Yoko's diary and he gathered contributions from old school friends and family to provide some background to Yoko's short life and to document the wider effect the bomb had on the families who survived.

Until this time Yoko's diary has never been published in English. I have added some information of my own in boxes throughout the text to explain aspects of Japanese life that would not be familiar to modern Western readers.

The diary is a class project and bears the stamp of a conscientious little girl who is always trying to do the right thing. She wants high marks for this work! She comes across as extremely diligent – whatever the circumstances – never questioning or disobeying. At home she seems a model child: always helping to prepare meals; helping her mother in the kitchen; helping wherever she can. 'I want to try hard and do my best every day,' she writes.

The reader might assume she was indeed such a very good girl. But that assumption should be taken with a grain of salt, given that the diary is a school project. Yet she does make some observations of historical interest. She records the war around her – the planes overhead, the chronic lack of food, the exhausting work, and her daily errands. We learn that the children had no holidays during the war – they even had to work on Sundays, gathering food and wood, labouring, and practising home defence in case the Americans invaded. Her little routine is laid bare.

Yet, despite this grim existence, Yoko always seems to find

something to be happy about: 'Today was the day of working at home. Yesterday my uncle came and so the house was very lively. I wished every day would be like that.' She writes this on 5 August 1945, the day before America dropped the atomic bomb on Hiroshima. Then her diary abruptly ends, silenced by the weapon to which she was horrifically exposed.

Yoko's story is one of many thousands. Nearly all of the students in her year at school, as well as their five teachers, died instantly in the atomic blast. They were among more than 6300 children who perished immediately. Others died of lingering wounds or radiation sickness.

Yoko's diary represents one Japanese girl's impressions of the world around her, at a time when that world was about to end. Yet if the Japanese regime treated her death as 'lighter than a feather' – as the Samurai code of *bushido* exhorted the Japanese people to view death – it was the heaviest thing on earth for her parents. According to Kohji, Yoko's mother never smiled again after she discovered her daughter's body.

This English translation of *Yoko's Diary* brings to a wider world the story of a young Japanese girl living in Hiroshima during the last months of the Pacific War.

Yoko was one of hundreds of thousands of innocent Japanese people who died or suffered from the world's first nuclear strike. Helping the survivors continues to this day, through the work of Nihon Hidankyō, the Japan Confederation of A- and H-Bomb Sufferers Organizations, which was awarded the 2024 Nobel Peace Prize, a long overdue, if fittingly timed, tribute on the eve of the eightieth anniversary of the nuclear attacks.

Moriwaki Family Tree

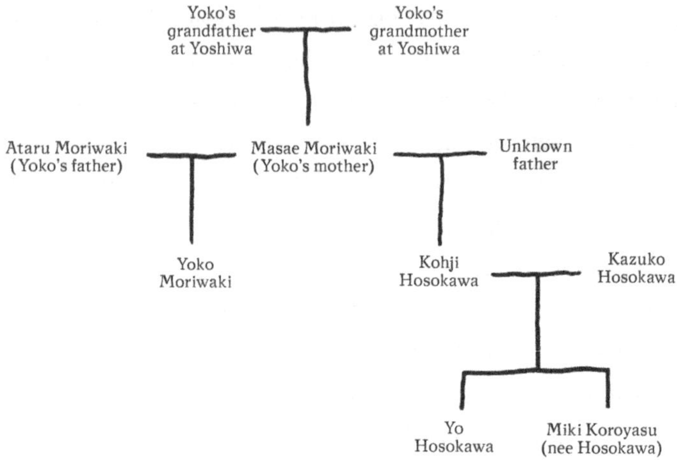

Other people in Yoko's life

Hatsue Ueda – nursed injured Yoko
Hiroshi Kamei – teacher from Hosei University Girls' High School
Kazuko Kojima (nee Fujita 'Fujita-san') – in the year above Yoko in school, travelled on ferry with her from Miyajima
Masafumi Yamazaki – recent Kenjo teacher who contributed to the book
Masako Kajiyama (nee Nakamoto) – one of few survivors from Yoko's class
Matsumoto-san – friend from Hatsukaichi
Okayama-san – Yoko's best friend from national school
Shizuko Oka ('Oka-san') – in the same year as Yoko, travelled on ferry with her from Miyajima
Yamashita-san – friend from Yawata

Teachers

Headmaster Oka – moral education and headmaster of Kenjo
Hori Sensei – mathematics
Kawakita Sensei – calligraphy
Kimura Sensei – biology
Kurita Sensei – physical science
Mitsuya Sensei – accompanied Yoko to Kannon Village School in Saeki District after the atomic bombing
Mizuiri Sensei – original homeroom teacher
Munekuni Sensei – practical studies
Nagahashi Sensei – music
Sasaki Sensei – geography and form master (Year 7), supervised students at Dobashi
Sekiyama Sensei – household management
Tsuji Sensei – Japanese
Tsukiji Sensei – replacement homeroom

Opening Yoko's diary

by Kohji Hosokawa

On 6 August 1945, Yoko Moriwaki, my little sister, bore the full brunt of the Hiroshima atomic bomb blast while she was doing housing demolition work in the Dobashi area, approximately 700 metres from the hypocentre (the point on the earth directly below the explosion in the air). That evening, at an evacuation centre located 10 kilometres away in the suburbs of Hiroshima, she passed away. She was thirteen years old. This book contains Yoko's diary.

The diary begins with the Kenjo school entrance ceremony. Yoko writes, 'The 1945 school entrance ceremony was held today. At last! I am now one of those girls I have long admired – a Kenjo student. I am going to be mindful of how I lead my daily life and work really hard so that I won't shame myself as a Japanese schoolgirl.'

Yoko's short sentences are overflowing with the joy she felt about entering high school, but the war quickly intrudes. One week later, she describes her shock and fear at having seen an enemy fighter plane for the first time. 'I saw one of those blasted B-29s for the first time today. It circled Hiroshima, trailing a long, beautiful contrail and then flew away.'

Yoko Moriwaki aged eleven. This picture was taken in 1944, the year before she entered Kenjo. (Kohji Hosokawa)

After that, B-29s would occasionally fly over Hiroshima and fly away without dropping any bombs. Now, when I think about it, I feel sure that they were monitoring the city in preparation for 6 August.

Day by day, Japan's war situation deteriorated and warning sirens became a daily occurrence. There was no time for classes; students were required to help in the war effort. I can almost see Yoko, gritting her teeth while labouring, trying to do her best, berating herself for feeling tired and comparing her situation 'to what our soldiers are going through ...' and 'to Father fighting in the war ...' and to the fierce battle 'being waged in Okinawa. I mustn't be outdone by the British and American schoolgirls ...'

As Japan entered the last days of the war, apart from those times when she travelled the long distance to and from school, Yoko had to go everywhere on foot. Whenever she did farm work at the Kenjo agricultural plot, demolition work, labour service or visited shrines to pray for the soldiers at war, she got there by foot. 'I went to Hara Village to help with farm work,' (round trip 16 kilometres) she writes on 11 June. Three days later she 'walked to Yoshijima Airport and planted sweet potatoes and soybeans,' (round trip 7 kilometres). But her tiredness catches up with her: 'We marched to Yagi Training Hall to put valuables belonging to the school in safe storage. On the way there, I simply wanted to throw them away! I did my best though,' (round trip 25 kilometres).

Sundays ceased to be holidays at that time, and the few days children had off were not called 'holidays', but 'days of working at home' or 'home training days', so that people would never forget that they were at war, even while they were resting at home. I counted the number of home training days that Yoko noted in her diary and compared them with the number of holidays Japanese schoolchildren have today. There were only twelve. Of course, there were no summer or public holidays either. In the same period today, Japanese schoolchildren have about forty days off including summer holidays.

Holidays were few, yet Yoko continued to toil with her malnourished, exhausted body in the midst of an extreme food shortage. In her diary, my little sister complains about her poor physical condition, saying, 'I have a fever ...', 'I feel sick ...', 'My whole body feels really weary.' As I read those words, I sighed heavily, because Yoko was not such a frail person by any means.

Our grandparents, who lived in the countryside, would occasionally attempt to supplement our diet, however slightly, sending rice, eggs and other things from their farm to Hatsukaichi, a market town which was 10 kilometres away across the sea from our home in Miyajima. They would mix such supplies with coal so that they could pass undetected beneath the watchful eye of the strict authority of the time. However, only the meagre amount of food that could be carried home by my mother and sister as they travelled from Hatsukaichi on the train and boat to Miyajima Island could ever reach us in this way. In her diary, Yoko sometimes mentions food, making comments such as, 'The *ohagi* sticky rice sweets were delicious,' or 'We ate peaches.' I vividly remember eating peaches with Yoko, as we hardly ever got to eat such things. When the peach season arrives each year, I remember that time and a lump forms in my throat.

Yoko records the first time she experienced planting rice at our grandparents' home. She felt so lonely being in the countryside far away from our mother and spent days impatiently waiting for Mother to come and get her. I really understand how she felt.

On those days that Yoko was able to attend school, we see her delighting in learning new things, as she looks up words in the dictionary, learns how to use a slide rule, peers through a microscope and makes her own summer uniform – in the lessons that weren't interrupted or cancelled due to air raids. The diary gives us a glimpse of young schoolgirls joyfully singing 'Natsu wa Kinu' (Summer is Coming) and rolling on the floor laughing at the funny stories told by their biology teacher, who must have been quite a character and features frequently in the diary.

They were very impressed when their household management teacher told them, 'One day you will be mothers and raise children. Teaching children manners is very important, you know.' But none of them would ever become mothers.

Once the student mobilisation order was issued, Yoko mentions the loneliness and even tension as, one by one, the older students were mobilised. She writes, 'Today, the Year 10 students were sent to the manufacturing battlefront. We will hold the fort while they are gone,' and 'We Year 7 students stood at the school gate and clapped as they left. I nearly started crying.' And later '... because only the Year 7 students are left now, the playground seems strangely bigger than before.'

Then the order was given for the Year 7 students to do labour service clearing away some houses that had been demolished. The area that was allocated to the Kenjo schoolgirls was Dobashi, a place close to the hypocentre of the atomic bomb, and 6 August was the first day of work.

As I read the diary, things that I had forgotten were among some of the small things that Yoko mentions in passing, and I was consumed by nostalgia. Yoko writes, 'I tied up my hair for the first time today.' I remember making fun of Yoko, telling her that, as she had forced her bob-length hair up with a band, it looked as if she had a small tail growing out of the back of her head.

'On the way home, the wind blew my hat into the sea. It is just too bad!' I will never forget Yoko's dejected expression as she said in a small voice, 'My poor hat! Floating all alone out there on the ocean.'

'I made dolls out of wool.' The two small dolls that Yoko made that day were kept in a doll case for a long time.

Yoko with her older brother, Kohji Hosokawa.

However, when my mother and father died, I placed one in each of their coffins.

At times, Yoko mentions that she has written letters to our father, who was away fighting in the war. Years later, after our father had been repatriated, I asked him about this and he told me that not one of Yoko's letters had reached him.

Here and there in the diary, we catch a glimpse of Yoko's sweet and gentle nature. 'I feel sorry for my classmate Hamada-san, whose father has died. I am going to comfort her.' Four months after Hamada-san's father died, she herself was killed by the atomic bomb.

'Today, a girl called Asako Fujita, who survived a major air raid on Osaka, joined our school. I am going to be her friend.' Asako Fujita survived the Osaka air raid only to be killed in Hiroshima by the atomic bomb. Many of the friends and teachers who feature in Yoko's diary were killed by the atomic bomb.

Then I was sent away to Kyushu on 12 June, just as air raids were becoming deadlier and more frequent, and Yoko, concerned about my safety, mentions that she prayed for me. 'God, please protect my brother Kohji.' I, for whom she prayed, was saved while she, who prayed for me, was killed.

What Yoko's diary taught me is that twelve- and thirteen-year-old schoolgirls had no idea that Japan's war defeat was imminent or that the remaining days of their own lives were numbered. Right until the very end they believed in their country. And above all, the diary tells us how cheerfully and valiantly they lived the days of their tragically short adolescence.

The last entry in Yoko's diary was written on 5 August, exactly four months from the date of the Kenjo school entrance ceremony. The following day, 6 August, the Year 7 Kenjo students met their fate in Dobashi. They had barely begun their demolition labour service when the atomic bomb exploded above their heads at 8.15am.

After the atomic explosion, my little sister was picked up by a relief truck and taken to a makeshift relief centre located 10 kilometres away. Critically injured, she died the same evening.

Report from Dobashi

On 6 August, approximately 220 Year 7 students were clearing away houses that had been demolished in the Dobashi area under the supervision of their form master, Kenichi Sasaki, and several other teachers.

The students gathered at Koamicho Tram Station at 7am to begin clearing away debris, such as tiles and pieces of wood. The first thing they did was to remove their school uniforms and change into light working clothes. They then placed their uniforms, together with their other belongings, such as bento boxes, in the shade of a row of trees. Afterwards, some of these uniforms and charred bento boxes were found and returned to the girls' families.

The students formed two lines and were passing tiles and other debris to one another relay-style when they met their fate. It is believed that most of the students and teachers died instantly and that the open space created by the demolished houses would have made the blast even more destructive.

The several dozen students who survived were instructed by their teacher to head to an evacuation centre in Koi. All of them were critically injured and by 7 August the following morning all had died.

According to reports made by the students before they died, Kenichi Sasaki, the teacher who had been supervising their work duties that day, sustained injuries to every part of his person including both of his legs, which were severely burned.

Despite this, the last instruction he ever gave his students was, 'I am done for. Everyone, head for the Koi evacuation centre!' He then drove his critically injured body forward through the flames to save his students and was never seen again.

The following day, Mr Sasaki's bag was the only trace of him found in the area.

Thus, all of the teachers and students who were at the school that day, and all of those who had been doing housing demolition work, ultimately perished.

Altogether, 297 Kenjo students and teachers were killed by the atomic bomb. Of these, twenty were teachers (including the school principal) and 277 were students.

Extract from the 1 March 1982 issue of the
Minami Yuho 80th Anniversary Commemorative Magazine
(Hiroshima Minami High School – predecessor of First
Hiroshima Prefectural Girls' High School or 'Kenjo')

Never spoken of, never forgotten

August 6, being a labour day for Yoko, meant her diary remained at home. Whenever I look at the diary that Yoko left behind, I am reminded of my mother who, during the remainder of her life, would read the diary alone, overcome with sadness. It was very difficult for me to see her like that, and so I would pretend that I didn't notice, and I did not open the diary for a very long time due to the sense of fear and distress I associated with it.

Eventually the diary came to the attention of the makers of a special NHK documentary entitled *Girls in*

Yoko with her father, Ataru Moriwaki, and her mother, Masae Moriwaki, in 1938.

Summer Dresses – Hiroshima – 6 August 1945, which told the story of the Year 7 students of Kenjo who were killed by the atomic bomb. Through this documentary, which was broadcast in August 1988, I met Hiroshi Kamei, a teacher from the Hosei University Girls' High School in Yokohama, who was coordinator of a special course for students about the atomic bombings. Each year the school conducted a four-day Hiroshima Study Trip, and on one such trip, at the pressing of the students, Mr Kamei tried to make contact with my father. My father was then in poor health so I offered to speak to the students in his place

Until then, I had barely mentioned to anyone the fact that I had experienced the atomic bomb and my sister had been killed by it; not because I was concealing the fact that I was a *hibakusha* ('atomic bomb survivor'), but because I did not want to remember it.

The meeting with Mr Kamei was a turning point in my life. I had always known that talking about the experience of the atomic bomb and leaving a record for future generations was the duty of *hibakusha*; but meeting him made me regret that I had avoided doing so. Now, every year on 6 August, I attend the memorial service for Kenjo A-bomb victims. The victims' parents who attend the ceremony are getting very old, and as the years pass their numbers grow fewer. And of course, there are no parents who can attend the ceremony for those schoolgirls whose entire families were wiped out by the bomb.

Hibakusha

Hibakusha – meaning literally 'bomb-affected people' – is the Japanese word for the survivors of the bomb. There were several hundred thousand survivors. Many were hit by flying debris. The flash and the firestorm burned others, and tens of thousands were exposed to potentially deadly radiation. Radiation poisoning was the most terrifying, because nobody understood the disease. The victims lost their hair, small purple spots appeared on their skin, and gradually they lost control of their bodies and died.

But many survived the poisoning to live out their lives with chronic health problems. Others were so badly deformed with burn scars called 'keloids' that they were shunned and forced to hide indoors by day. In many homes the parents of young *hibakusha* hid all the mirrors to spare the child the misery of seeing him- or herself. Many bomb-affected children refused to go to school because they were mocked as 'red demons' and 'monsters'.

All *hibakusha* were, at first, treated as outcasts in Japanese society, rather like lepers. But gradually efforts were made to help them, and today special hospitals and nursing homes treat the survivors.

PH

I began this mission too late in life, so the time that remains is very precious to me. For that reason, I now tell my story every year to Hosei University Girls' High School students who visit Hiroshima on their annual Hiroshima Study Trip.

One such time, Mr Kamei took Yoko's diary in his hands and urged me to have it published, saying, 'This precious record must be left behind.'

At the very least, it is a diary from the era when, in the last days of World War II, Japan was in the grip of a severe food shortage.

Kohji Hosokawa with his wife, Kazuko Hosokawa, and (centre) Masako Kajiyama, who was in the same class at Kenjo as Yoko, and was involved in the publishing of Yoko's Diary *in Japan in 1996.*

The paper quality is poor, the ink has faded, and the diary itself is quite badly damaged. Realising that I could delay no longer, I sat down at my computer. The task I had set myself forced me to type the words of my little sister's diary into my PC. It was an extremely painful task, which I did with a heavy heart.

Nevertheless, as I turned the pages, a strange thing happened – my sweet, gentle little sister came back to life before my eyes, and my emotion changed from one of heavy-heartedness to one of nostalgia. I felt as if we were having a conversation. One by one, the diary brought things that I had forgotten flooding back to me, and quite to my surprise it warmed my heart.

The hole that Yoko left

by Miki Koroyasu

Whoever would have thought my father had so many memories buried deep inside him?

He had always been hesitant to talk about the atomic bomb and his sister, Yoko, but the thing that changed all that was the NHK production *Girls in Summer Dresses*, which was broadcast on 7 August 1988. He later told me that he had been unable to sleep that night. Necessity forced him to read his sister's diary.

Ever since I was a child, I had found it strange that my father never spoke publicly about his experience of the atomic bomb. Now I saw him completely immersed in the task of painstakingly revealing, piece by piece, that part of his past he had been most loath to remember. I guess it took fifty years before he could finally bring himself to talk about it.

My grandmother also hardly ever mentioned Yoko or her life around the time of the atomic bomb. But shortly before she died, she did tell me something that I will never forget as long as I live.

After being repatriated from China, my grandfather finally arrived home one day to find my grandmother gaunt and emaciated, her grief at Yoko's death having robbed her of the very will to live. She tried to tell him what had happened to Yoko, but as she tried to move her mouth, her voice and strength both failed her and she found she was unable to speak. My grandfather reassured her, 'You don't have to tell me.' He then ran her a hot bath and bathed her emaciated body. She told me that she was deeply comforted by that act of kindness.

I have been told that when I was a newborn baby, my grandfather, who was a music teacher and who had inspired Yoko to dream of being a musician, would sit at my bedside, his mind awash with memories of his daughter, and play the harmonica to me. Both my grandfather and grandmother were delighted when I quite unwittingly decided to pursue a career in music.

One thing I remember vividly is my grandmother bringing me a box of tomatoes which she had carried home

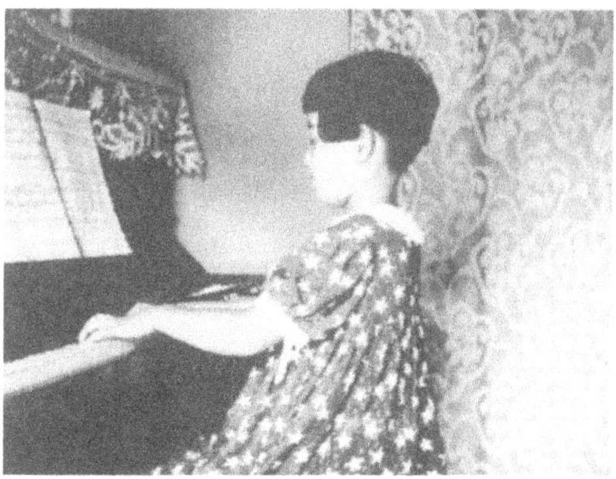

Yoko playing the piano at home in 1943. (Kohji Hosokawa)

from the market. It was a hot summer day, about one year before my university entrance exams, and the sun was beating down mercilessly. The box was huge and crammed to the top with rows of delicious-looking bright red-ripe tomatoes. Goodness knows how heavy it must have been! My grandmother was sweating and panting with exertion. The tomatoes were gleaming in the summer sunlight, and the sight of them suddenly reminded me of Yoko's necklace of red beads, which I used to call 'rubies' even though they were really made of glass. It dawned on me that my grandmother really wanted to give those tomatoes to Yoko, who had loved tomatoes.

Now Yoko's diary has been published. I believe that the aspect of Yoko's diary that people find most appealing and powerful is that it is a faithful record of facts.

These unadorned facts are passed on to the next generation, unfaded by the passage of time. This, I believe, is the mission that is demanded of us, the ones left behind.

Second-generation hibakusha

by Yo Hosokawa

When I was a small child, my parents would occasionally take me to Hiroshima to visit my grandparents. Hanging in the cool, dark entranceway of their home was a picture of a young girl. For a very long time, I found the gaze of that girl, who always seemed to be looking my way and smiling faintly, quite unnerving. After all, I was just a young lad.

For as long as I can remember, 6 August has been a somewhat special day for me. In the morning our family would visit Peace Park, folding our hands together in prayer before the numerous monuments. We would also sing songs at various ceremonies we attended, such as the memorial service for Kenjo atomic bomb victims. In the evening, we would stand on the bank of the Motoyasu River and pray as countless lanterns drifted by on the current. Although I never consciously thought of the day as being either special or normal, 6 August was for me, I suppose, a day when our family normally did special things.

As I grew older, I changed schools several times, as my father moved around a lot with his job. I was surprised

A portrait of Yoko by Kenzo Oya, which hung over a doorway in Yoko's parents' house. (Kohji Hosokawa)

to learn that in other prefectures what was a normal thing for me was not normal for others. This prompted me to go around telling people about the Hiroshima holocaust. I was now acutely aware of the fact that I was a second-generation Hiroshima survivor. Despite that, I knew virtually nothing about the atomic bombing of Nagasaki, and made no effort to learn about it.

As I moved to different cities and schools every couple of years, I developed a strange feeling that because I was a second-generation Hiroshima survivor, and therefore hadn't experienced the atomic bomb myself, I didn't really belong to either world – the world of Hiroshima or the world outside. This feeling for a long time both sustained and tormented me.

My father has occasionally talked to me about his experience of being an atomic bomb survivor. Even when I was only a child, it was obvious to me that the experience had completely shattered his whole world, so much so that it was difficult for him to describe. As a child, I listened grave-faced whenever he told me those grim stories. Before long, I also became aware that the story told by my father and that told by my mother held different nuances.

I had not heard my father tell Yoko's story all that often, and when he did, he did not provide many details. Most of what he has ever told me about Yoko was triggered by Yoko's diary, which even I saw only for the first time when I was working on tasks related to the publication of this book.

Perhaps for my father the atomic bomb and especially Yoko are now like a part of himself. Although my father began speaking about the atomic bomb, and finally Yoko, as he started to age, he has still never spoken to me even once about his inner self.

When my child was diagnosed at a young age with a sarcoma, I suspected it was linked to my being a second-generation atomic bomb survivor. Even though there is no scientific proof of it, I feel in my bones that the two things must be linked. As my child gets older, I notice the resemblance to my father in everything from his features to his personality, and to me this reinforces the fact that my mother's and father's blood flows in his veins.

I guess that for me, thinking about the atomic bomb means thinking about its impact on my identity and family, before considering the past mistakes made by Japan or world peace.

My grandmother passed away fifteen years ago and my grandfather followed two years ago. Whenever I visit their home, I feel as though two people who should be there are missing. For my grandparents, I suppose the young girl in the picture was always the person who should have been there.

My parents now live in that home. Today, it seems they live more freely, selfishly and with more regard for themselves than they ever could have in the past. The picture of the young girl still hangs in the home my parents settled in after many years of constantly moving around. For my father, I believe she will always be the one who should be there. Naturally, that girl is still looking my way and smiling faintly. Only now I don't find the feeling that she is watching me unpleasant. She will remain a young girl forever.

Even though I am now an adult, my parents continue to worry about me. But I believe that Yoko, although far away, is watching over me.

Little sisters

by Kazuko Hosokawa

Yoko Moriwaki is my older sister-in-law whom I never met. And Yoko's father, Ataru Moriwaki, is my former music tutor. Yoko's dream of following in her father's footsteps by pursuing a career in music was cruelly ripped away by the atomic bomb. After the war, by some twist of fate, I began to learn the piano from Mr Moriwaki. At that time, I was about the same age as Yoko had been when she died.

My husband and I share a common experience in that we both lost our younger sisters, who can never be replaced, to the atomic bomb. Although we were aware of this fact before we got married, for some reason we never broached the subject with one another; perhaps there was some unspoken agreement between us not to do so. But on the eve of the publication of this book, my husband began furiously writing down all of his memories of Yoko, something he had so determinedly avoided doing in the past.

As I watched him in this task, I was filled with a deep sadness because it stirred up vivid memories of my own younger sister, Fumiko.

In 1944, my family left Tokyo, where air raids were becoming deadlier and more frequent, and evacuated to my grandparents' homes in Hiroshima. For various reasons, temporarily my younger brother and I stayed with my mother's parents in Hatsukaichi, while my younger sister stayed with my father's parents in Enomachi, Hiroshima.

In the spring of 1945, my younger sister started her first year of national school. On 6 August, the day of the atomic bomb, she was at Hirose National School, located only 600 metres from the hypocentre, coincidentally in the same vicinity as Dobashi, the area where Yoko was when she was bombed.

I believe that Fumiko was fatally burnt by the sudden wave of intense heat and thrown by the sheer force of the blast. Meanwhile, my grandmother on my father's side somehow managed to crawl from the ruins of her home and run to the school to look for Fumiko. In the ensuing chaos, she was unable to find her, and in a deeply distressed state she narrowly escaped death herself by running to my mother's parents' house.

On 7 August, Fumiko was found crouched near the household drinking fountain, her body charred black. My small sister had used the very last of her strength to make her way home, only to be engulfed by the raging inferno when she got there. We could faintly make out the letters of her name on a fragment of clothing that had been spared by the flames. She was only five years old.

My grandmother, who doted on her like no other, passed away one month later, on 5 September. At the time it was as if she had followed Fumiko to the grave to be with her. Although she didn't have any obvious physical injuries, my grandmother's hair fell out and her whole body became covered in red marks – typical symptoms of radiation sickness.

The Pacific War broke out a short time after my younger sister was born. More timid than most children her age, she would always don an air-raid hood, grab her first-aid bag and take cover immediately at the sound of an air-raid siren. During wartime blackouts, she was petrified that lamplight from inside the house would shine outside, and she would cry out in a shrill voice that was close to a scream, 'Quick! Turn out the lights!' Terrified of air raids and always exceedingly cautious during one, my younger sister didn't stand a chance in the atomic bomb attack.

Even though her body had been found, it took a very long time for me to accept the fact that my younger sister had died. For years I waited for her to return, half expecting that she would suddenly reappear one day, laughing and calling out, 'Smile!' Even today, I clearly remember the innocent, cheerful expression on her face when we parted for the last time.

Medical Treatment of the Hibakusha

Immediately after the end of the war, the *hibakusha* – or survivors of the bomb – received little medical treatment. The reason is because the medical teams arriving with the occupying Americans were instructed to study the effects of radiation on the human body, not help the survivors.

Caring for the wounded was the job of the city's own doctors and nurses. But many of these had been killed in the bombing, so Hiroshima had to rely on help from other cities. However, those doctors had to care for their own sick, and the medical teams that did come were unable to meet the huge demand for help anyway. The occupying forces also refused to supply much medicine. They claimed it was not their responsibility.

Some American doctors were shocked by their orders, but most decided that experimentation on the victims would be of great value to medical science. That was true, and we certainly learned much about radiation poisoning from the Japanese victims of the bomb. Still, the medical teams failed to help thousands of people desperately in need.

As the years passed, American doctors did try to help the victims, offering plastic surgery and other services for free in several cases. And visiting foreign doctors often did their best to assist the survivors.

PH

It is cruelly ironic that my father's mother and my younger sister evacuated to Hiroshima only to be killed by the atomic bomb. Even today my heart aches when I think about my small sister's tragic death.

Every year on the night of 6 August, rows of lanterns resembling a multitude of red sashes float down the Motoyasu River, where the A-Bomb Dome casts its reflection. Flowing silently among the sashes, which represent the memories of so many people, are Morinaga milk caramel candies – an old Japanese favourite – packaged in their traditional yellow box.

The A-Bomb Dome, left as a memorial to the Hiroshima bombing, by the Motoyasu River. (Kohji Hosokawa)

My husband's and my own younger sisters both died without ever eating candies. These sweets are a small prayer-filled offering to all of the small children who perished that day.

Even though fifty years have passed since the end of that insane war, time has not healed Hiroshima's grief and suffering.

I am now older than my grandmother was, and my grandchildren are the same age as my younger sister. For their sake, I must do my part to help preserve peace.

Back at Kenjo

For the short time she was a Kenjo student, Yoko would travel to school from Miyajima with Kazuko Fujita, who was one year above Yoko, and with Shizuko Oka, who was in the same year. Kazuko remembers that time here.

Memories of that time

Back then, most people in Hiroshima called First Hiroshima Prefectural Girls' High School 'Kenjo', and the school had an image that was steeped in rich history and tradition.

Yoko Moriwaki was a new student in 1945, which marked the forty-fifth year since the school's foundation. Both Yoko and Shizuko Oka, who had attended the same national [primary] school in Miyajima as Yoko, passed the tough entrance examination and arrived at Kenjo full of excitement about attending such a prestigious school. By that time, all of the senior students had been mobilised to work in factories, so there were only three of us travelling to school each day from the small island of Miyajima. But then in mid-July, the Year 8 students, of which I was one, were also given a mobilisation

Miyajima

Yoko lived on the beautiful, green island of Miyajima, one of Japan's most sacred sites, about 20 kilometres from Hiroshima by ferry and train. Miyajima means 'shrine island', after the great religious shrine that has stood there for centuries. It is mountainous and covered in maple trees; in autumn they fade and turn the whole island bright crimson.

Since 1168 – for almost 1000 years – a huge *torii* gate has stood on the sand in the bay. According to the Japanese faith called Shinto, a *torii* gate marks the visitors' entrance to a sacred space. It announces the worshippers' arrival at the shrine. The *torii* gate typically comprises two giant posts with a cross bar. The magnificent gate at Yoko's home island is a giant orange structure standing 16 metres tall. The present gate was erected in 1875, and seems to rise out of the sea at high tide. It would have been the most striking thing that Yoko saw as she set off for school each morning on the ten-minute ferry ride she took to the mainland.

PH

order and so the three of us travelled to school together for only a brief period – just over three months.

Together we would take a ferry to the port of Miyajimaguchi, where we would change to a suburban train bound for the city. From there, we walked forty minutes to school. We must have been a strange sight, a group of students clattering along the street in our wooden *geta* sandals, dressed in baggy trousers made from old clothes or our mothers' kimonos, en route to school. Students from other schools often called ours 'the rag school', and I suppose they were right. At that time, our school had been partially converted into a school factory, which served as a military clothing depot. There was a teacher shortage, and we frequently had to take cover in bomb shelters on the way to school due to air raids.

Perhaps out of concern for the students' safety, school attendance was divided into two blocks – the morning group and the afternoon group; there were few formal classes. We students worked at the school's agricultural plot, dug bomb shelters and carried stones from the upper reaches of the Ota River on a *mocco* – a piece of cloth with handle hooks on the corners – which was carried between several people like a stretcher. The stones were placed inside the bomb shelters to fortify them.

In classes, we would often prepare 'comfort parcels' containing daily necessities, food and confectionery, or handmade fans, with accompanying letters for our soldiers serving at the front.

Lunchtime was our respite from the daily grind, a time when worries were forgotten. Yoko, Shizuko and I would often return to Miyajimaguchi and eat lunch together from our bento boxes, sitting on the jetty with our legs dangling over the edge, gazing out across Hiroshima Bay at Miyajima Island. One such time, a single green pea rolled out of my bento box and sank into the clear ocean below, as the three of us watched it intently. 'Shall I drop another?' A second pea disappeared into the beautiful water and we followed it with our eyes, like people observing a strange spectacle. For some reason, that unremarkable moment, the green colour of those peas, remains vividly etched in my memory.

I don't remember having much to do with those two girls while we were at national school. I was one year older than they were and did not live near them. But I remember Yoko as being a cute girl – humorous, plump and fair-skinned, while Shizuko was a slender beauty with a narrow face. Although each was the only child in her household, both seemed confident in front of people and I believe they studied hard. I was very surprised a few years ago by a photograph my younger sister sent me of the three of us. At one time, we were all shrine maidens of the Itsukushima Shrine on Miyajima. Because of the manpower shortage, national school students were sent to stand in for regular shrine maidens at festivals, under the instruction of their schools. I'm not sure how we would have looked, dancing in our red pleated skirts and waving bells, but we all did our best. I had forgotten all about it, but the three of us shared such an experience.

My younger sister says that she really respected and admired Yoko. As the war raged on, national school students would go to the jetty to welcome the souls of departed war heroes back to the island. Everyone would sing a song called 'Mugon no Gaisen' (Silent Triumph) about the soul of a dead soldier returning home. We practised that song every day. It began with Yoko singing solo, but then the choir would join in.

This picture was taken in 1944 when Yoko and her friends were shrine maidens of the Itsukushima Shrine; Kazuko Fujita is in the centre and Yoko at the far right.

Shrine Maidens

Shrine maidens, known in Japan as *miko,* are young women who perform the services of junior priestesses, or shamans, in Shinto ceremonies. They have appeared in Shinto religious rites since ancient times, often in ecstatic trances to amaze the nobility. Their more modern tasks include sacred dancing (the *kagura*), ritual cleansing, chanting and driving out evil spirits with various implements, such as a bow, a supernatural box (which traditionally contained animal and human skulls) and *sakaki* tree branches.

The shrine maidens then and now typically wear long red trousers or pleated skirts, a white jacket and red hair ribbons – white and red being the traditional Shinto colours (and colours of the Japanese flag). Some *miko* were entitled to speak on behalf of the spirits of the dead, and were characterised in popular Japanese culture as witches. But these days most are young women who perform the rituals of the Shinto faith, like an altar boy in a Christian service.

PH

Soaring in the clouds and mountains over the horizon
A man who defeated the enemy
Returned home today in silence

My younger sister told me that Yoko's beautiful voice and commanding presence would send her into a reverie. Later, not long after Yoko entered Kenjo, she apparently surprised my sister by saying, 'Fujita-san, do come to Kenjo next year!' Yoko absolutely loved Kenjo, and these words are testament to her kindness, her pride as a student of that school, and her self-confidence. The following year, my sister managed to be admitted to Kenjo, but Yoko would never know of her delight at this achievement, nor hear her words of gratitude.

On 6 August, the day of the atomic bomb, I was at Hiroshima Air Base where I had been mobilised to work. The signs of Japan's imminent defeat were becoming more apparent by the day, and we were no longer charged with the task of making propellers from duralumin. All we did each day was to practise honing cutting tools. At 8.15 that morning, a great flash illuminated the eastern sky, and the windows of our building glowed red. A moment later, we heard a deafening roar. With no idea what had happened, we escaped by crawling on our hands and knees to a low hill that everyone called Biwayama (Loquat Hill) because it was covered in loquat trees. At first, we all thought that the factory had been hit by a bomb or an incendiary weapon. Meanwhile, downtown Hiroshima was in the grip of a catastrophic disaster. No reliable information reached us at Biwayama for quite some time. Full of foreboding, we simply watched the eastern sky as it went through weird changes.

'Whatever has become of the Year 7 students who waved to us from outside the train this morning?' These words escaping our teacher Kimura Sensei's lips were like a cry of distress.

After a while, black rain began to fall from the sky over the mountain.

Yoko's body was brought home by her mother the next day. Hearing what had happened, I rushed to her home, but there was nothing I could do. I did remove my Kenjo school badge and pin it to Yoko's chest, but I couldn't bring myself to look at her face or touch her.

Fifty years have passed since that day; time moves inexorably forward. But in my heart, Yoko will always be the kind, sincere, smiling young girl that I remember.

– Kazuko Kojima (nee Fujita), former student of First Hiroshima Prefectural Girls' High School (Kenjo)

On 6 August, Masako Nakamoto did not go to do labouring in Dobashi because she was recovering from an operation. She is one of the very few girls in Yoko's year at Kenjo who narrowly avoided being victims of the atomic bomb.

My friends etched in stone

We entered Kenjo in the spring of 1945, aged twelve years old. At that time we had no way of knowing that the atomic bomb would be dropped a few months later and the war would come to an end.

Unlike the Year 7 students, who wore a mismatched combination of ragged attire due to the harsh wartime conditions, the senior students wore the navy blue sailor-suit summer uniform – the collar of which was edged with a double white line. They stood in rows at the entrance ceremony without so much as a hair out of place, welcoming us. We were all so proud to be admitted to Kenjo, so we made sure we sang the school song, 'Spring Hills', as beautifully as we could.

Kenjo was located in the centre of Hiroshima. Here and there, places along the route to school were plastered with posters proclaiming the 'The Final Battle for the Homeland'. Before long, news of the Battle of Okinawa reached us, and one after another Japanese cities were burned to the ground in incendiary bomb attacks launched by B-29s. Then in July, the Year 8 students were mobilised and sent to work in factories, so the Year 7 students, who were the only students left at the school, had a lot of labour service to do cultivating land at the East Drill Ground, planting potatoes at Yoshijima airport and clearing away demolished houses.

One such day, I was diagnosed with acute appendicitis and hospitalised at the Shima Hospital, which stood right at the hypocentre, very close to the Hiroshima Prefectural Industry Promotion Hall (the present A-bomb Dome). The air raid on nearby Kure occurred on the second day of my hospitalisation, on 2 July, and I remember gripping the hand of my mother, who was beside herself with fear, in the darkness of a wartime blackout while the sirens clamoured around us. The fateful day of 6 August came in the days after I left the hospital, while I was still not feeling one hundred per cent. On that day I stayed at home and studied instead of labouring in Dobashi.

That day my classmates were burned to death (most of them died instantly) in the intense wave of heat that radiated from the atomic explosion while they were working in Dobashi, a place devoid of any shelter whatsoever. By the next day, the few students who had managed to escape through the burning city by heading towards Koi and were picked up by trucks and taken to relief centres had all passed away.

Meanwhile everyone who was at Kenjo that day, including Headmaster Oka and one class of senior students (a nursing class), perished.

Today, tucked away in a small pocket of the downtown high-rise area on one side of leafy Heiwa-Dori Street stands the Kenjo School Monument. Until the morning of 6 August, our school had occupied the same site. A Japanese wisteria tree stood at the southern end of the gymnasium in the school yard. Only a few months earlier, its purple flowers had fluttered in the May breezes. Even now, I can hear my friends' murmuring voices as they stood under that wisteria tree in a circle around the water taps, where we would enjoy a cool drink after doing labouring work.

The names of Yoko Moriwaki, who left us the diary, and the classmates with whom she joyfully sang 'Summer is Coming' are all engraved on that monument. All of those children will remain just twelve or thirteen years old forever.

The names of places such as Heiwa Koen (Peace Park) and Heiwa Ohashi (Peace Bridge) resonate with the underlying sadness inherent in the Japanese word *heiwa* ('peace').

Once again this year, the Kenjo School Monument, which bears the names of Headmaster Oka and the twenty teachers and 277 students who were victims of the atomic bomb, is soaked by the early summer rain. The outstretched branches of a large Japanese wax tree that towers over the monument tell the story of the years that have passed since that day.

Half a century on, Japanese schoolchildren visit Hiroshima on school excursions. As I stand beside the monument and talk to them about 'that day', I hear the schoolgirls whispering and see my classmates, whose lives were suddenly extinguished.

I will never stop coming here to pray about that day.

My life and the diary of a girl who died on 6 August overlap.
With my finger I trace the place where my name should be
among those etched here in rows
the names of those whose remains were never found.

Friends killed by the atomic bomb sleep forever in this
monument made from star dust.
Yoko Moriwaki sang 'Summer is Coming' but was killed
shortly after by the atomic bomb;
here she sleeps, her memory etched in stone.

– Taken from the anthology *Hanadokei* (The Flower Clock) by Masako Kajiyama (nee Nakamoto), a former student of First Hiroshima Prefectural Girls' High School (Kenjo)

The Kenjo School Monument. (Kohji Hosokawa)

The diary of Yoko Moriwaki

RUSSIA
MANCHUKUO
(Japanese - occupied Manchuria)
Vladivostok
Sea of Japan
Peking
KOREA
JAPAN
Tokyo
Hiroshima
Osaka
CHINA
Nagasaki
Shanghai
US Navy Blockade of Japan
N
W
E
S
PACIFIC
OCEAN
Hong Kong
Philippine Sea
Manila
South China Sea
PHILIPPINES
Japan in the Pacific
July, 1945
Scale
0
500
1000
Kilometres

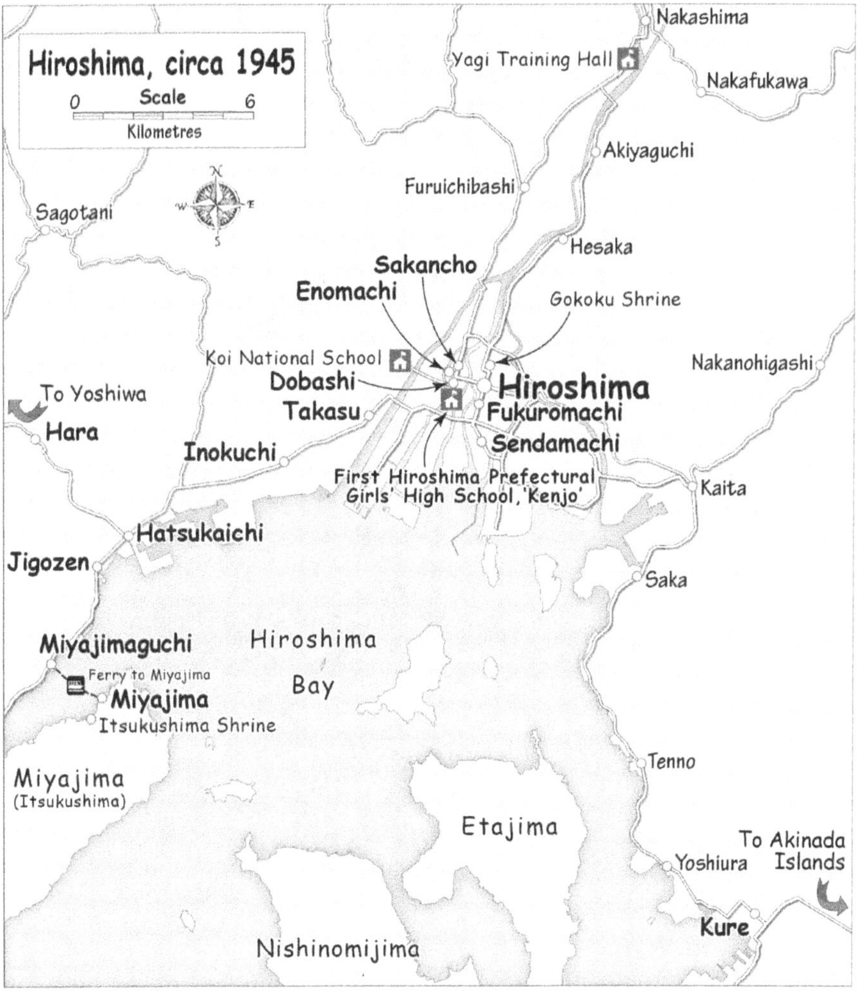

Hiroshima, circa 1945
0
Scale
6
Kilometres
N
W
E
S
Nakashima
Yagi Training Hall
Nakafukawa
Akiyaguchi
Furuichibashi
Sagotani
Hesaka
Sakancho
Enomachi
Gokoku Shrine
Koi National School
Nakanohigashi
Dobashi
Hiroshima
To Yoshiwa
Takasu
Fukuromachi
Hara
Inokuchi
Sendamachi
First Hiroshima Prefectural
Girls' High School, 'Kenjo'
Kaita
Hatsukaichi
Jigozen
Saka
Miyajimaguchi
Hiroshima
Bay
Ferry to Miyajima
Miyajima
Itsukushima Shrine
Tenno
Miyajima
(Itsukushima)
Etajima
To Akinada
Islands
Yoshiura
Kure
Nishinomijima

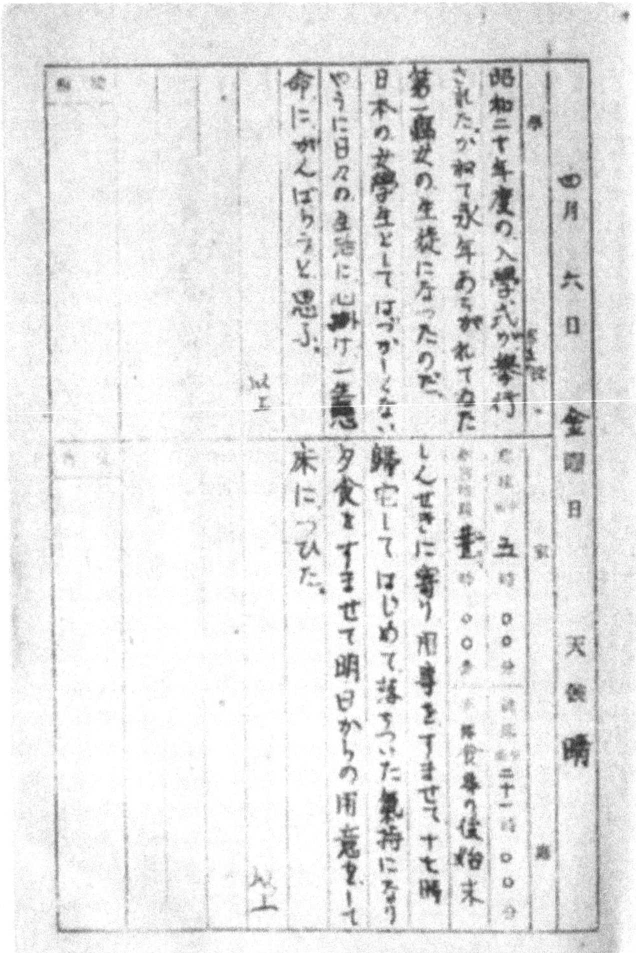

四月 六日 金曜日 天候 晴

學校

昭和二十年度の入學式が擧行
された、かねて永年あこがれてゐた
第一高女の生徒になったのだ、
日本の女學生としてはづかしくない
やうに日々の生活に心掛け一生懸
命にがんばらうと思ふ。

以上

家庭

起床時 五時 〇〇分 就寝時 二十一時 〇〇分
勉強時間 壹時 〇〇分 手傳 食事の後始末

しんせきに寄り用事をすませて十七時
歸宅してはじめて落ちついた氣持になり
夕食をすませて明日からの用意をして
床につひた。

以上

Yoko's diary entry for 6 April, the day of the Kenjo school entrance ceremony. (Kohji Hosokawa)

April

6 April (Fri) Weather: fine

School

The 1945 school entrance ceremony was held today. At last! I am now one of those girls I have long admired – a Kenjo student. I am going to be mindful of how I lead my daily life and work really hard so that I won't shame myself as a Japanese schoolgirl.

Home

I visited our relatives on an errand and returned home at 5pm. On arriving, I felt calm and relaxed for the first time today. I ate dinner, prepared the things that I will need from tomorrow and went to bed.

Woke up: 5am **Went to bed:** 9pm **Study:** none **Chores:** washed up after dinner

7 April (Sat) Weather: cloudy

School

Today the new students met the senior students. The senior students were so inspiring, and I have decided that I am going to do my very best in everything so that I don't damage the Kenjo school spirit.

Otsuka Sensei, who has taught the senior students since 1943, retired today. I do not know what kind of a teacher he was because he never taught me, but I joined in and gave him a hearty send-off anyway.

Home

Today was the first day of school. In the morning, I sprang out of bed, bursting with energy. If Father were here, he would have been overjoyed! I must to do my best for him, as well. Father, please be happy today, because I was made deputy class captain of Class 6!

Woke up: 5.30am **Went to bed:** 9pm **Study:** 30 minutes **Chores:** prepared dinner

---

School Pride

Yoko's school was called the First Hiroshima Prefectural Girls' High School, or Daiichikenjo ('Kenjo'). It stood in lush green grounds near Dobashi, about 700 metres west of the city centre, which was the target for the atomic bomb. As one of the city's oldest and most prestigious schools, First Hiroshima was very hard to get into: Yoko had to sit a difficult test and all the students were carefully selected. It was a bit like our selective high schools.

In his contribution to the Japanese edition of this book, Masafumi Yamazaki, a teacher at Kenjo, wrote: 'Its ethos was teaching girls to become good wives and wise mothers who possessed great fortitude and perseverance and were frugal and steadfast. In spite of the strict educational policies it maintained, the school also focused on sports, music and extracurricular activities, besides the pursuit of knowledge, and it produced valuable, contributing members of society.'

Yoko performed well and was delighted to be named a Kenjo student, and therefore be considered a clever or wise girl. Certainly she was very obedient and always seemed to be striving to improve herself, to meet the standards she thought her parents and teachers had set for her. Unsurprisingly she became deputy class captain.

PH

8 April (Sun) Weather: rain then cloudy

School

Today was an Imperial Rescript Proclamation Day and home training day.

Home

I woke up later than usual this morning because my legs were tired from 5 April, when I walked all the way home from Yoshiwa, which is about 23.5 kilometres inland. My old national [primary] school teacher, Yoshikawa Sensei, has been transferred to an external position, so I gave him a farewell present. Yoshikawa Sensei was a very kind, interesting teacher who was good at drawing. Farewell, Yoshikawa Sensei.

Woke up: 7am **Went to bed:** 9pm **Study:** 1 hour **Chores:** prepared dinner

Getting Around

As Japan's losses mounted and Allied aircraft struck deep into the homeland, the basic services of Japanese society collapsed. Telephone services were severely disrupted, and often areas of the city and surrounding villages relied on a single communal phone. Train services between towns were very infrequent. But inside Hiroshima, the people prided themselves on their excellent inner-city tram service, which continued through the worst of the war – and resumed just days after the atomic bomb fell.

Nevertheless, Yoko found herself having to walk long distances to and from her home, as did many other Japanese children who had to make their way to schools or factories, farms or demolition sites. Yoko often mentions walks of more than 20 kilometres. That's like walking Sydney's City to Surf race twice a day.

Her fellow student Kazuko Fujita mentions in her 'Memories of that time' how she and Yoko and Yoko's classmate Shizuko Oka caught a ferry, a train and then walked for forty minutes to get from Miyajima to school.

PH

9 April (Mon) Weather: rain then cloudy

School

While we were in the gymnasium today, we were told what to do when we hear a warning siren. At the sound of a siren we must go straight home. Area groups were also announced for people who cannot return home because they live too far away. Before we were sent away, our names, addresses and telephone numbers were taken down so that our families can be contacted at such times.

Home

Yesterday was Sunday so I wasn't really in the mood for working; but I pulled myself together straight away when I got to school and saw the headmaster and the teachers.

Next week I will be more careful.

This evening I wrote to Father and told him that I had been made deputy class captain. He will be so happy when he gets the letter.

Woke up: 5am **Went to bed:** 9pm **Study:** 30 minutes **Chores:** prepared dinner

Letters to the Soldiers

Yoko wrote several letters to her father, but none of them reached him. His whereabouts were unknown – the family believed only that he was fighting somewhere in the Pacific. Japanese children did occasionally receive letters from their fathers or brothers serving abroad, but these were heavily censored by army officials. Any mention of their suffering or location was cut out. To reveal a soldier's location to his family was considered a security risk.

Only good news was allowed to be written in letters sent home. So the families were being told that the Japanese soldiers, sailors and airman were doing well in the war and victory was theirs – when in fact they were on the verge of complete defeat.

PH

10 April (Tue) Weather: rain

School

Today was the first day of actual classes. In our first and second lesson hours we learned sewing. In the third hour we studied national literature. In the fourth hour we did drawing. In the fifth hour we studied etiquette.

I was surprised to find that these subjects are taught in a completely different way from how they were taught at national school. I must make sure I do a good job in these classes.

Home

Today was a gloomy, rainy day.

When I got home from school, one of my relatives, Aki, had come to see us. Aki is a fourth grade student at Fukuromachi National School, and is going to be evacuated to Futami District. I feel sorry for her having to live so far away from her parents. But it will all be worth it when we win the war. Aki, don't lose heart!!

Woke up: 5am **Went to bed:** 10pm **Study:** 1 hour **Chores:** prepared dinner

---

Evacuees

To escape the danger of the firebombing that was occurring all over Japan, children between the ages of four and twelve were evacuated from the cities to the countryside.

In 1945 about 23,500 Hiroshiman children were evacuated. One was a little boy called Shoso Kawamoto. His experience was typical. While his parents and most of his family stayed in Hiroshima to work, Shoso travelled by train with hundreds of other classmates to a village about 50 kilometres away. When he arrived, he and his friends slept on straw *tatami* mats on the floor of a local Buddhist temple. They got a bowl of rice for breakfast and a bowl of rice for dinner. There were no lights at night. The youngest children were terrified of their strange new surroundings and the long dark nights, and they wet their beds and cried, for which they were bullied by the older kids.

The older kids soon abandoned their classes to join the local boys in gathering wood, digging for pine roots and stealing food. In time, these evacuated children formed gangs, made slingshots and went hunting in the forests. Once a month their parents visited. 'We would spend just a few minutes together,' Shoso remembered, years later. His parents always left with a prayer that he would return safely to Hiroshima.

Shoso survived the war in his village, but his parents in Hiroshima died in the bombing.

PH

11 April (Wed) Weather: rain then fine

School

Today we learned a subject called household management for the first time. It is very interesting and I like it a lot.

I heard that the father of Hamada-san, one of the girls in our class, passed away. I feel so sorry for her. Next time she comes to school I am going to go right over and comfort her.

Home

I am going to do my homework now, which is to make a table of my daily chores. Hmm, I wonder what kind of a table I will make ...

Today I borrowed some books from Ishikawa-san, who is a student at Shintoku Girls' School. I am so excited! Now that I have books, I am going to work really hard.

Woke up: 5am **Went to bed:** 10pm **Study:** 1 hour **Chores:** prepared dinner

---

曜/時	1	2	3	4	5	6
月	歴	体	数	國		
火	實	々	地	國		
水	数	國	修	歴		
木	数	裁	物	々		
金	裁	々	音	國		
土	家	々	書	生		

Year 7 Timetable. (Kohji Hosokawa)

Day / Lesson	Mon	Tues	Wed	Thurs	Fri	Sat
1	History	Practical Studies	Mathematics	Mathematics	Dressmaking	Household Management
2	Gym	Practical Studies	National Language	Dressmaking	Dressmaking	Household Management
3	Mathematics	Geography	National Moral Education	Physics	Music	Calligraphy
4	National Language	National Language	History	Physics	National Language	Biology

12 April (Thu) Weather: fine

School

Today we did warning-siren evacuation drills in our first lesson hour. The first time it took six minutes for us to evacuate, but the second time it took only four. When you evacuate, the most important thing is to be swift and silent.

In the afternoon, I was playing in the school yard when the warning siren sounded again, so I came straight home.

Home

The warning siren sounded, so I visited our relatives and waited at their home until it went off. Then I returned home with Mother on the 5.47pm ferry. When we got there, my uncle had come to see us.

I prepared my things for tomorrow and went to bed.

Woke up: 5am **Went to bed:** 10pm **Study:** 1 hour **Chores:** prepared dinner

Warning Sirens

An air-raid warning siren sounded whenever an American aircraft was spotted flying over the city. The Japanese people nicknamed the B-29 bombers B-san, which literally means 'Mr B'. The people would scurry to bomb shelters – often just holes in the floors of their homes, or shafts in the dirt – and hide from an expected attack. They would wait until a second siren sounded the 'all clear' and then emerge from the shelters and resume their work. But there were many false alarms. It usually just meant a single American bomber was overhead, which mysteriously flew around then left. Little did the Japanese realise that these planes were reconnaissance flights, sent months ahead of the mission to drop the atomic bomb.

Some planes were on training exercises and dropped dummy bombs called 'pumpkins' in the surrounding countryside. One plane at a time seemed harmless. Most Japanese cities had been attacked by waves of bombers – up to 150 at a time – and soon the people of Hiroshima ignored the sirens completely. Yoko herself heard the sirens on several occasions and hid in a bomb shelter with her fellow students. But one thing puzzled the people of Hiroshima: already American bombers had destroyed so many Japanese cities. Why was their city being spared?

PH

13 April (Fri) Weather: fine

School

I saw one of those blasted B-29s for the first time today. It circled Hiroshima, trailing a long, beautiful contrail, and then flew away. The warning siren sounded again today, so I was back home again by lunchtime.

Home

Everyone is buzzing with the news of seeing the scary B-29. When I got home, I had lunch and went to Tamada Sensei's house. Tamada Sensei is a teacher at Miyajima National School. Tomorrow, he will join the Kure City Marine Corps [the naval corps that trained conscripted and volunteer soldiers]. He is probably worried about his family. So that Father won't worry, I am going to help Mother and do my best every day.

Woke up: 5am **Went to bed:** 11.30pm **Study:** 1 hour **Chores:** helped to prepare meals and ran an errand

14 April (Sat) Weather: fine

School

Today we did labouring work in our first and second lesson hours. Demolition work on the gymnasium has started, so we carried the scrap wood to the back garden.

Mizuiri Sensei, our homeroom teacher, returned from Hiroshima today.

Home

Today Tamada Sensei finally left to go and fight in the war. He seemed to be in a very good mood. When I asked Shoji, who is still very small, 'Where is your daddy?' he replied proudly, 'Daddy went away in a train. He is a soldier, you know.' I feel sorry for him being so far away from his daddy when he is so small.

Woke up: 5am **Went to bed:** 9pm **Study:** 1 hour **Chores:** prepared meals

---

Child Labour

In April 1945 Yoko and her friends heard from their teachers that children aged twelve and older would have to join the war effort as student labour. This was because the National Mobilisation Law – compelling all adults to work in war industries – was extended to children.

Until they were assigned duties in factories, offices, munitions works, or labouring, students worked in the school agricultural plots or on whatever jobs came up around the school. Yoko mentions cleaning kitchens and removing rubble, and her school friend Kazuko Fujita recalls digging bomb shelters and filling them with rocks from the Ota River.

PH

15 April (Sun) Weather: fine

School

Today at school we laboured until lunchtime. In the afternoon, we studied. The headmaster talked to us about posture and breathing.

There was also an orientation for new students. The sun was beating down and it was terribly hot, but we put up with the heat and got through it.

Home

A lot of rations arrived today – matches, shellfish and vegetables. Because it was my family's turn to distribute the rations, I helped too. My legs were a little tired from all that walking, but I finished everything I had to do quickly and then went to bed.

Woke up: 5am **Went to bed:** 9pm **Study:** 1 hour **Chores:** helped distribute rations

Rationing

Japan was running out of everything, not just food. Families had to donate metal in their homes to arms factories to be turned into bullets and parts for aircraft. There was little coal or oil, so their homes had to rely on wood fires. Children took one bath a week in freezing water, because they hadn't the fuel to heat the baths. The government insisted on very strict food rationing: food was limited to rice and potatoes, and it had to go a long way. Anyone showing off their money was frowned upon. Women who wore brightly coloured kimonos were mocked.

Many child labourers got sick or collapsed from exhaustion. Even though she rarely complains about shortages, Yoko did suffer from extreme tiredness and dizziness, possibly due to overwork and a lack of food.

Families tried to help each other and formed little neighbourhood groups which shared food and clothing and wood. Farmers were expected to send food to the cities. If you were lucky enough to know a farmer, you could hope for more food than other people. Luckily, Yoko's grandparents were farmers.

Gradually people realised that the US naval blockade was slowly choking and starving the nation. American war ships surrounding the country sank any Japanese ships trying to bring supplies or reinforcements home.

16 April (Mon) Weather: fine

School

Today the warning siren sounded in playtime after our second lesson hour, so I came straight home.

Home

My whole body felt really weary and I also had a fever and a headache, so I went to bed early.

Woke up: 5am **Went to bed:** 8pm **Study:** 30 minutes **Chores:** prepared meals

17 April (Tue) Weather: fine

School

Today I had a slight headache and didn't really enjoy eating the food in my bento box. My tonsils feel swollen.

The warning siren sounded during cleaning time, so I came straight home on the 4.02pm ferry.

Home

My headache got even worse after I got home, but I just put up with it. I went to bed early after reviewing the work we will do in tomorrow's lessons and practising my calligraphy.

Makoto Mizuiri is my new homeroom teacher.

Woke up: 5am **Went to bed:** 9pm **Study:** 30 minutes **Chores:** prepared meals

18 April (Wed) Weather: fine

School

The warning siren sounded again today but it stopped almost straight away.

Kawakita Sensei scolded me in calligraphy class because I wasn't meditating as I was rubbing down my ink stick on the ink stone. [Students meditated to calm their minds so their calligraphy would turn out well.] I will make sure I do a superb job in his next class.

Home

Woke up: 5am **Went to bed:** 10pm **Study:** 30 minutes **Chores:** prepared meals

---

The warning siren sounded so I visited our relatives, the Murakamis. I wasn't able to let my teacher know, so I told the leader of the group I walk to school with, and she said I could go.

Wartime Discipline

Japanese schools in the 1940s were like little military camps, and as much of the instruction was to train students for their role in the war as it was to educate them. Part of that training was to instil in them a love of the empire and the Emperor. Obedience and discipline were essential to that. Boys were beaten, whipped or slapped for the slightest offence. Girls were not to question anything.

Children like Yoko just did as they were told. Older ones were taught how to use bamboo spears and drilled to defend the motherland from an American invasion. Government advertisements urged boys to take to the sky as *kamikaze* pilots, who flew their planes into enemy ships. It was all part of a massive government campaign to train Japanese people to be willing to fight to the death for the homeland.

PH

19 April (Thu) Weather: rain then cloudy

School

I rested at home because I was ill.

Home

I have been overdoing it a bit lately, so I couldn't go to school today. I had a sore throat and lost my voice, and my head, arms and legs felt terribly weary. I really wanted to go to school but I simply couldn't.

Woke up: 6am **Went to bed:** 8pm **Study:** 30 minutes **Chores:** prepared meals

20 April (Fri) Weather: fine then rainy then fine again

School

Because I rested yesterday my body felt slightly weary today.

Tsuji Sensei taught us how to look up words in the dictionary, and Kurita Sensei taught us physical science, which was very interesting.

Home

Today, my older brother, Kohji, came to see us, so the whole house felt very festive. Because it's always just Mother and me, we tend to get a bit lonely. But it will all be worth it when we win the war. Father, please do your best!

Woke up: 5.20am **Went to bed:** 9pm **Study:** 1 hour **Chores:** prepared meals

21 April (Sat) Weather: fine

School

Today, a new student called Asako Fujita joined our class. She is an evacuee from Osaka. She was still in Osaka when ninety of those B-29s attacked the city and will be coming to school every day from Jigozen. I am going to be her friend.

Home

I started to do my homework as soon as I got home, but then realised I had forgotten how to make a dress pattern. I went to see Oka-san and asked her how to do it, and then did it myself.

Woke up: 5am **Went to bed:** 8pm **Study:** 1 hour **Chores:** prepared dinner

Attacks on Tokyo, Osaka and Other Japanese Cities

In March 1945, the people of Hiroshima heard via radio, newspapers and rumour what had become of Tokyo, Osaka and other major Japanese cities. On the ninth of that month, Tokyo experienced the worst ever air raid on a city in human history: more than 100,000 people died in a single night after 325 American bombers dropped almost half a million canisters of jellied petroleum on the civilian areas. The canisters burst into flames on impact, and the result was a firestorm that made Tokyo look like the crater of an active volcano.

Osaka, Japan's second largest city, was next. On 13 March, American planes firebombed Osaka, with a population of more than three million. The aircraft flew in low and dropped their incendiary load over the surburban areas. The pilots didn't even aim for the big war factories on the outskirts of the city. About 4000 people died and many more would have died had they not been evacuated prior to the attack. Osaka was subsequently bombed seven times. The city was devastated and residential areas were completely flattened.

Usually the cities were warned of approaching raids. American pilots would drop pamphlets telling people to evacuate their cities. And there were sirens. A typical raid involved more than a hundred planes.

PH

22 April (Sun) Weather: fine

School

Today was a home training day.

Home

Today Matsuno Sensei, who taught me when I was in fifth grade at national school, visited my home. We talked about all sorts of things and he gave me a fountain pen. My older brother and his friends took apart a gramophone and fixed a lot of parts that were broken. Where there is a will there is a way!

Woke up: 6am **Went to bed:** 9pm **Study:** 1 hour **Chores:** prepared dinner

---

Home Training Days

On weekends and some weekdays, Japanese children and their parents were expected to train for the possibility of an American land invasion. In mid-1945, the country expected the Americans to come at any time. American ships surrounded Japan and American aircraft controlled the air. Nothing could get in or out of the country, and food supplies were rapidly running out. The government in Tokyo ordered the people to prepare to defend their cities and homes. On training days, women and girls were told to attend classes in self-defence and taught how to use bamboo spears. They also learned how to put out fires, build bomb shelters, and provide basic medical care.

PH

23 April (Mon) Weather: fine

School

Today we learned mathematics in our first lesson hour. We started learning how to use a slide rule. It seems very interesting. The warning siren sounded about halfway through our fifth lesson hour, so I came straight home.

Home

Mother was distributing firewood rations when I got home, so I helped her. I studied, read a book for a while, ate dinner, did some sewing, practised doing abacus calculations, wrote my diary and went to bed.

Woke up: 5am **Went to bed:** 9pm **Study:** 1 hour **Chores:** prepared dinner and helped distribute rations

24 April (Tue) Weather: fine

School

Today a farewell ceremony was held for Kawakami Sensei and Okamoto Sensei. Kawakami Sensei has been transferred to Hatsukaichi Industrial High School, and Okamoto Sensei has been transferred to the Hiroshima Municipal Shipbuilding Technical School. It is too bad I never had the chance to learn from them.

Home

In the train on the way to school today I started to feel sick. My body felt slightly weary today as well. Lately, I have been feeling tired and weak, so I must make sure I do my exercises.

Woke up: 5am **Went to bed:** 10pm **Study:** 1 hour **Chores:** prepared dinner

25 April (Wed) Weather: fine

School

In our household management class today, we learned about having respect for the elderly.

Elderly people have spent most of their lives working for the good of the nation and their families, and we would not be here today if it were not for them. We should take very good care of them, as one day they will be our ancestors who will protect and bless us.

Today's lesson really made sense to me and I think it was very important and useful.

Home

The warning siren sounded this afternoon so I returned home on the 3.16pm ferry. I heard that a large airplane had invaded the airspace above Akinada. On the way home, I heard a loud boom. I wonder what it was ...

Woke up: 5.30am **Went to bed:** 9pm **Study:** 1 hour **Chores:** prepared dinner

---

Japanese Cultural Attitudes to the Elderly

Elderly people, and especially old men, were expected to be treated with deep respect. This was part of a long Japanese tradition which honoured the village elder or the local chief or warlord. In traditional Japan, older men were seen as deserving of admiration for their experience and wisdom – even if the old man wasn't always wise or experienced, or, by their life's example, they didn't deserve the honour. This attitude of respect for the elderly was stronger in wartime Japan, which was an authoritarian, militaristic society ruled by old men.

Six men – members of the military and prominent Japanese politicians – ruled the country in 1945. Emperor Hirohito was largely a figurehead ruler who could intervene as a last resort. In the last days of the war, the 'Big Six' decided that Japan would never surrender to America unless America promised to preserve the life of Emperor Hirohito. They were quite willing to lead their country to a bloody end in defence of the Emperor. They saw nothing wrong in ordering the Japanese people to give their lives for this goal – even when they knew that Japan was defeated. Most ordinary people seemed to accept this fate. Many saw the destruction of their country as a great act of self-sacrifice in the name of their spiritual leader, the Emperor.

PH

26 April (Thu) Weather: fine

School

Today we learned biology for the first time. Our biology teacher is Kimura Sensei and he is a really interesting teacher. We learned about pine tree pollen and could see it very clearly when we looked at it through the microscope.

Home

The air-raid warning siren sounded this morning, so I thought about coming back home, but in the end I went to school.

Somehow I managed to catch the 4.02pm ferry today. Normally I arrive at the terminal too late to catch it. After I got home I studied, wrote my diary and went to bed.

Woke up: 5am **Went to bed:** 9pm **Study:** 1 hour **Chores:** prepared dinner

---

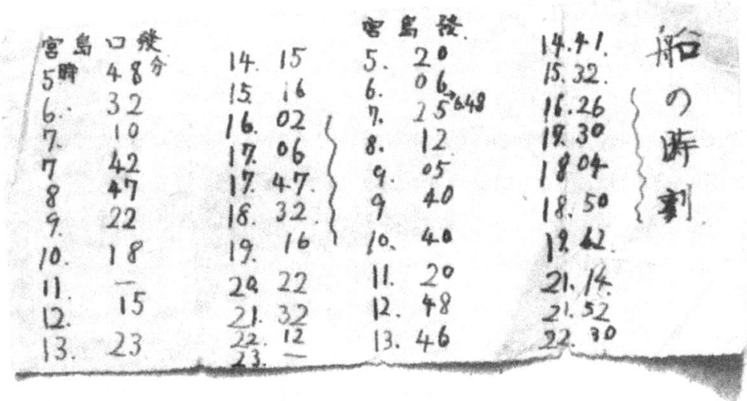
船の時刻

宮島口発
5時 48分
6. 32
7. 10
7 42
8 47
9. 22
10. 18
11. —
12. 15
13. 23
14. 15
15. 16
16. 02
17. 06
17. 47.
18. 32.
19. 16
20. 22
21. 32
22. 12
23. —

宮島発.
5. 20
6. 06 → 6.48
7. 25
8. 12
9. 05
9 40
10. 40
11. 20
12. 48
13. 46
14.41.
15. 32.
16. 26
17. 30
18 04
18. 50
19. 42.
21. 14.
21. 52
22. 30

(Top) The ferry timetable made by Yoko and (bottom) 'Misenmaru', the ferry Yoko took when she travelled to school. (Kohji Hosokawa)

27 April (Fri) Weather: fine then a little rain then fine again

School

Today in physical science class we learned about gas. Gas is poisonous, so we must check the gas pipe thoroughly for holes or cracks. The warning siren sounded towards the end of our fifth lesson hour, so I caught the 3.16pm ferry home.

Home

The warning siren sounded today, so I came home earlier than usual. I reviewed what I learned today at school and prepared for tomorrow's classes.

I also tied up my hair for the first time today. I did my sewing homework, wrote my diary, filled in my table of chores and went to bed.

Woke up: 5.20am **Went to bed:** 9pm **Study:** 1 hour **Chores:** prepared dinner

28 April (Sat) Weather: fine

School

Today we went to work at the Kenjo agricultural plot in Takeyacho in our first and second lesson hours. We broke the ground with hoes and pulled up grass before returning to school. The warning siren sounded soon after we got back, so I caught the 12.15pm ferry home.

Home

I came home earlier than usual today because there was a warning siren.

I ran various errands and studied. I also chopped some wood. When I was chopping, the axe struck my left index finger. I gasped! But luckily I wasn't hurt.

Woke up: 5am **Went to bed:** 9pm **Study:** 1 hour **Chores:** prepared dinner, helped run errands, chopped wood

---

Agricultural Plots

The severe food shortage forced every Japanese family to grow food. Little market gardens and agricultural plots sprang up all over the city. School playgrounds became veggie gardens; backyards were taken over with crops. The schoolchildren were expected to tend their playground farms, as well as plots elsewhere, and come in daily to perform this job. The crush of small homes in the centre of Hiroshima made it very difficult to grow anything there. But the Japanese were adept at squeezing organic life out of the tiniest spaces in order to survive.

Yoko worked at Kenjo's agricultural plot in Takeyacho, a short distance from the school, as well as on farms at nearby villages. She also worked at her grandparents' farm at Yoshiwa, during an extended visit there.

PH

29 April (Sun) Weather: fine

School

Today is Tenchosetsu – the forty-fourth birthday of our Emperor. At school, we celebrated with a ceremony that started at 9am. Halfway through the ceremony the warning siren sounded, so we finished up quickly and went home.

Home

On the way home I went to see Matsumoto-san, who lives in Hatsukaichi. She gave me a bento box and we went to a field and picked things like mugwort and lotus flowers. After that, I caught the 5.47pm ferry home.

Woke up: 6am **Went to bed:** 9pm **Study:** 1 hour **Chores:** prepared dinner

Tenchosetsu

Tenchosetsu is the Japanese word for the Emperor's birthday. During Hirohito's reign, it was celebrated on 29 April.

In peacetime the Emperor would usually appear on the balcony of the Imperial Palace in Tokyo, ride his horse in public, or walk among the people to celebrate his birthday. But during wartime this was too dangerous and he stayed indoors – or in his bomb shelter, a spacious underground apartment beneath the Imperial Palace. Of course, in those days it was highly unusual to see the Emperor of Japan in the flesh. He was regarded as a living deity, or god, and believed to be descended from the Sun Goddess. The military government was determined that he should not diminish himself by getting too close to the people. So Hirohito maintained a dignified distance to perpetuate the myth of his holiness. The people weren't allowed to refer to him by his name. They called him the Sacred Crane.

The day remains a national holiday and is called Showa Day, after the name given to Hirohito's reign.

PH

30 April (Mon) Weather: fine

School

Today, a B-29 bombed the Shirakamisha Shrine area. Although the resulting damage was very minor, we must not underestimate the power of even a single enemy fighter.

On this day last year, Father received his military call-up notice.

Home

The warning siren sounded so I headed straight home. Mother was visiting a relative and so I told that to the leader of the group I walk to school with and she allowed me to go to our relative's home instead.

On the way home, Mother and I stopped by Jigozen, where Grandfather had gone to get his tooth fixed. Then we all caught the 7.18pm ferry back home together.

Woke up: 5.20am **Went to bed:** 9pm **Study:** 30 minutes **Chores:** prepared dinner

---

May

1 May (Tue) Weather: rain

School

Today the Year 10 students were sent to the manufacturing battlefront, so we gave them a hearty send-off. About 200 were sent to Toyo Industries and another 150 or so were sent to Hiroshima Air Base, in accordance with the mobilisation order. We must hold the fort while they are gone and make sure we work just as hard as they do.

Home

Woke up: 5.20am **Went to bed:** 9pm **Study:** 1 hour **Chores:** prepared dinner

There was a teachers' meeting today, so we studied for two hours before cleaning up and going home. Because I got home earlier than usual, I rested for a little while and then ran an errand. I practised my calligraphy, prepared for tomorrow's classes, wrote my diary, filled in my table of chores and went to bed.

The Manufacturing Battlefront

Since April 1945 when the Student Mobilisation Law was applied, schoolchildren were gradually assigned to the manufacturing battlefront. The Year 7 students at Yoko's school continued to work on farm plots and other cleaning jobs, and also to receive some lessons. Senior students, including the Year 10s, were mobilised to work full-time in munitions factories, on factory lines or in clerical roles. Women without work were pressed into serving in the Women's Emergency Labour Corps, which had about twelve million female members.

Most children were proud of their strange new role: they would be joining the adults and working to save the country. Some, like Yoko – who loved going to school – were perhaps disappointed and nervous, but still resolute. And some brave teachers dared to disagree with the new government order, which forced school students to work in areas that were at risk of aerial bombardment by American planes. But Japanese people were expected to obey the government without question.

PH

2 May (Wed) Weather: fine

School

In our household management class today we learned how to take care of our little brothers and sisters. The things that humans need above all in order to live are food, clothing, shelter, sleep, air and sunlight.

One day we are going to be mothers managing our own households and even raising children, so we all worked hard in today's class.

Home

I returned home on the 5.06pm ferry. Mother was preparing dinner when I got there, so I stepped out to buy some miso. After dinner, Mother and I discussed all sorts of things. After that, I wrote my diary, filled in my table of chores, wrote a letter to Father and went to bed.

Woke up: 5.20am **Went to bed:** 9pm **Study:** 1 hour **Chores:** prepared dinner, ran an errand

---

3 May (Thu) Weather: fine

School

Kimura Sensei's biology class was our first lesson of the day.

Kimura Sensei is a really funny teacher and today he was talking about beggars. He was so hilarious we couldn't stop laughing.

We also learned how to do multiplication using a slide rule. About halfway through our fifth lesson hour, the warning siren sounded and so I caught the 3.16pm ferry home.

Home

I came home earlier than usual because there was a warning siren. When I got home, Mother still hadn't returned from seeing the dentist, so I went to meet her at the jetty (she was on the 5pm ferry) and we came home together. I finished dinner early, wrote my diary and filled in my table of chores before going to bed.

Woke up: 5.20am **Went to bed:** 9pm **Study:** 1 hour **Chores:** prepared dinner

---

4 May (Fri) Weather: fine then rain

School

The warning siren sounded just as the teacher was about to hand back our diaries, so he couldn't return them to us. I have forgotten a few things, so I will just write up to here today.

Home

As I mentioned before, I don't really remember what I did today, so I won't write anything.

Woke up: 5.20am **Went to bed:** 9pm **Study:** 1 hour **Chores:** prepared dinner

---

5 May (Sat) Weather: fine

School

I came home early today because the warning siren sounded in our third lesson hour. We all took cover straight away. I heard that an enemy bomber attacked the area around the Fukushima Bridge.

Home

I got home earlier than usual and visited my old national school on an errand for the headmaster. I was really happy to see some of my old national school friends there.

On this day last year, Father left to fight in the war.

Woke up: 5.20am **Went to bed:** 9pm **Study:** 1 hour **Chores:** prepared dinner and ran an errand

---

6 May (Sun) Weather: fine

School

Today we had a mathematics test in our first lesson hour. Our second lesson hour was calligraphy, so we practised writing the character for 'heart'. Our third lesson hour was gym, but I came home early when a B-29 flew over Hiroshima, setting off a warning siren during play time after our second lesson hour.

Home

After I got home I had dinner and rested for a little while. After that, Mother showed me how to knit a cord for my jacket. It was fun!

I finished my national language homework, wrote in my diary, filled in my table of chores and went to bed.

Woke up: 5.20am **Went to bed:** 9pm **Study:** 1 hour **Chores:** prepared dinner

---

7 May (Mon) Weather: fine

School

From today our class will be divided into two groups. We practised how to take cover in an air raid. My group will take cover in bomb shelter number one. School finished at lunchtime, so I came home on the 2.16pm ferry.

Home

I will be coming home from school earlier from now on. I got home, studied and did some more knitting on my jacket cord. Dinner was still some time away, so I went outside and played football.

Woke up: 5.20am **Went to bed:** 9pm **Study:** 1 hour **Chores:** prepared dinner

8 May (Tue) Weather: fine

School

Today is Imperial Rescript Proclamation Day. At school we flew the national flag, had a ceremony and listened to a reading of the Imperial Rescript on the Declaration of War. The warning siren sounded, so we all took cover straight away. I heard that fifteen or sixteen planes flew over Hiroshima.

Home

I came home on the 2.16pm ferry. After resting for a little while, I did some more knitting on my jacket cord. Then I did my homework, reviewed what I learned today at school, prepared for tomorrow's classes, wrote my diary and filled in my table of chores.

Woke up: 5.20am **Went to bed:** 9pm **Study:** 1 hour **Chores:** prepared dinner

Imperial Rescript Proclamation Day

In 1942 the government declared the eighth day of each month to be Imperial Rescript Proclamation Day, in commemoration of the Imperial Proclamation of the War Against Britain and America on 8 December 1941, the day after the Japanese raid on Pearl Harbor and the start of war with Britain and America. On this day newspapers would reprint the Proclamation on their front pages and families would fly the Japanese flag over their homes. At school, children participated in special ceremonies, read from the Proclamation and honoured the soldiers fighting in the war.

The day was all part of the government's determined effort to maintain nationalist fervour and prepare children for fighting the enemy in an invasion. Those efforts were successful, as we hear in Yoko's comments throughout her diary. For example, she writes on 5 June: 'We are pushing forward on that battlefield, striving to increase production. If we will not work hard, who will? Whatever it takes, we must work as hard as we can until we win the war.'

9 May (Wed) Weather: fine

School

Our national moral education teacher was away today, so the headmaster came and talked to us instead. In mathematics we practised doing multiplication and division.

Home

I got home, ran an errand and then went with Mother to Hatsukaichi to pick up some charcoal that my grandparents sent us from their home in the countryside. Then we rested at Matsumoto-san's house before catching the 8.12pm ferry home.

Woke up: 5.20am **Went to bed:** 10pm **Study:** 1 hour **Chores:** ran an errand and prepared dinner

10 May (Thu) Weather: fine

School

Today the warning siren sounded in Tenmacho and the air-raid siren sounded in Sakancho, so we went straight to school and took cover there. We were in the bomb shelter for four hours, so I was a bit tired. But whatever happens, I must not give up.

Home

On the way home I went to see our relatives the Murakamis and also visited the Yamaguchis, who live in front of Jissen Girls' School. When I got to Miyajimaguchi, the ferry had just left. It was too bad! I visited the Kawaras and rested at their home before catching the 5.06pm ferry home.

Woke up: 5.20am **Went to bed:** 9pm **Study:** 1 hour **Chores:** prepared dinner

Opposite: *The Miyajima jetty and the 'Misenmaru' ferry. Yoko travelled to and from school each day via this jetty. (Kohji Hosokawa)*

Some School Rules

The following rules were recorded in the students' classroom diary:

- We must not run in the corridor.
- We must not enter the classroom wearing *geta* sandals.
- Cleaning should be done in silence.
- We must not simply stand around chatting all day.
- We were very noisy when we went inside the bomb shelter. We must do it more quietly in future.
- I think we are too noisy when we are doing private study in the classroom. We must remind one another to exercise a little more restraint.

– Collated by Masafumi Yamazaki, later a teacher at Kenjo

11 May (Fri) Weather: cloudy then fine then rain

School

The air-raid siren sounded as soon as I got to school today, so I took cover in the bomb shelter. After a while, the siren ended and I was just thinking about going back home when another warning siren sounded so I took cover again straight away. After that siren went off, I caught the 11am ferry home.

Home

I had lunch and rested for a while. While we were making emergency rations, Mother suddenly came down with a stomach-ache, so I took care of her and prepared dinner. I was really happy because she praised me and said I did a great job.

Woke up: 5.30am **Went to bed:** 9pm **Study:** 1 hour **Chores:** prepared meals

---

12 May (Sat) Weather: fine

School

I had such a good day at school today. Our biology teacher is really funny. He said, 'Who wears the best clothes at Kenjo?' and everyone burst out laughing.

Home

I came home on the 2.20pm ferry and then went to play at Kosuga-san's house. Kosuga-san's older sister who went to Osaka has come home.

Woke up: 5.20am **Went to bed:** 9pm **Study:** 1 hour **Chores:** prepared dinner

---

Smart Uniforms

While the senior girls, when they had been at school, wore the typical sailor suit uniforms, junior students wore any mismatched combination of clothes or the hated *monpe* – grey trousers and tunic and sandals. Some girls made dresses and headbands out of their mother's kimonos, and changed into their *monpe* at school or work.

'We must have been a strange sight, a group of students clattering along the street in our wooden *geta* sandals, dressed in baggy trousers made from old clothes or our mothers' kimonos, en route to school. Students from other schools often called ours "the rag school", and I suppose they were right. At that time, our school had been partially converted into a school factory, which served as a military clothing depot,' recalled Yoko's fellow student Kazuko Fujita.

PH

13 May (Sun) Weather: fine

School

Today was a home training day.

Home

I overslept a little this morning because I have been getting up so early every day. I prepared for my classes and Mother made me some *ohagi* sticky-rice sweets for lunch.

Yokoshima-san had promised that she would come to see me today, but she didn't. There was a warning siren, so that is probably why she couldn't make it.

Woke up: 8.30am **Went to bed:** 9pm **Study:** 1 hour **Chores:** prepared dinner

14 May (Mon) Weather: fine then cloudy

School

In our mathematics class today, we practised doing division with a slide rule and completed some of the exercises in the book. A new teacher called Tsukiji Sensei conducted gym class. We practised dodging things and walking in pitch darkness.

Home

On the way home I stopped by the public hall to see several things that had come from the Grumman American fighter airplane and were on display. Some of them were really amazing, but on the whole I was disgusted by how horrible they were.

Woke up: 5.20am **Went to bed:** 9pm **Study:** 1 hour **Chores:** prepared dinner

---

What Children Knew About the War

Japanese schoolchildren knew how it felt to live in constant fear of air attack; many had seen their cities attacked by US bombers. They were also taught to hate the Americans and British. Some chanted slogans, fed to them by the government. For example, children sang 'Kill the Americans and British one, two, three,' as they worked clearing building debris in Hiroshima. Children were taught to blame all their discomforts on the enemy. The lack of food, the evacuation drill, the interrupted school classes – all were blamed on the enemy.

Yoko writes, on 5 June, 'I am sure British and American schoolgirls are working hard doing all sorts of things to win the war. We must not be outdone by those schoolgirls, we simply mustn't.'

Her counterparts in Britain and America weren't labouring for the war effort like Japanese schoolgirls at all.

PH

15 May (Tue) Weather: rain

School

I will be in the afternoon group from today. It feels quite strange. We took cover twice when the warning siren sounded. We did two hours of practical studies [agriculture] and then cleaned up, before I caught the 5.06 ferry home.

Home

I came home and helped Mother prepare dinner. Mother is doing some sewing at the moment, so I helped her by cutting threads and winding them up. I filled in my table of chores, wrote my diary, prepared for tomorrow's classes and went to bed.

Woke up: 5.30am **Went to bed:** 9pm **Study:** 1 hour **Chores:** prepared dinner

---

16 May (Wed) Weather: fine

School

Today we practised using a slide rule and did some exercises in the book. The warning siren sounded during national language time, so we took cover straight away. Sasaki Sensei sent us a message to let us know that we will start doing demolition work tomorrow, so we went home.

Home

Because I came home on the 5.17pm ferry, Mother had already prepared dinner and was waiting for me. Today, Mizuiri Sensei told us to ask our parents where the word *aho* [silly] came from. So after dinner I asked Mother but she didn't know. When I told her where it came from, she said, 'I see.'

Woke up: 7am **Went to bed:** 9pm **Study:** 1 hour **Chores:** cleared away after dinner

A Different Syllabus

Many of Yoko's classes were interrupted by air raids or replaced by labouring work at the school's agricultural plots, cleaning around the school, and later demolition work in the suburbs.

When the classes did occur she took great pleasure in them. Some of the lessons seem strange by today's standards. Household management classes prepared the girls for their roles as wives and mothers. Practical studies involved learning about agriculture and commerce.

Yoko seems very excited when she gets to use a slide rule, which is an instrument like a little ruler-calculator with a standard set of scales marked on it that can be slid into position to answer a maths problem. National literature would have involved learning patriotic texts and symbolism associated with the empire.

PH

17 May (Thu) Weather: fine

School

Labour service began today, at last.

Our job is to clear away seventy buildings, starting with the local courthouse. Most of the rubble has already been cleared away, but I am going to work hard and do the best job I can anyway.

Home

My legs were quite sore after today's labour service, but who cares about that compared to what our soldiers are going through. I resolved to work hard again tomorrow, and wrote my diary, filled in my table of chores and went to bed.

Woke up: 5.30am **Went to bed:** 9pm **Study:** 1 hour **Chores:** prepared dinner

Exhausting Work

In Hiroshima, as in other cities, the children's jobs were exhausting. Yoko and her classmates were required to help clear away house tiles and debris that lay on the ground after houses surrounding important buildings had been demolished to create firebreaks – long, wide avenues, which were meant to stop the spread of fires that were expected after American bombing raids. Japanese homes burned very easily. They were usually made of stiff paper, like cardboard, and caught fire like dry wood.

Many children worked long hours. Some rose at 4am to do household chores before school or mobilisation duties; in the evening, they would resume their chores until late. Often they were sent into the forest to gather food – berries and wild fruit – or to collect wood and pine roots. The wood was actually used in aeroplanes, because Japan had almost run out of steel, and the pine roots were ground into oil, which would be used as fuel.

The Student Mobilisation Order insisted that all children over twelve should work as hard as adults. It was little wonder that girls like Yoko – the youngest of the mobilised children – felt exhausted and dizzy. Millions of Japanese children were overworked and undernourished during the war years.

PH

18 May (Fri) Weather: fine

School

I did labour service again today. Just as I thought, we were clearing away rubble in the same area as yesterday. I cut my hand while I was dragging some bamboo along. It was only a small cut but it hurt a lot. But who cares about that compared to the battlefield.

Home

I returned home on the 5.47pm ferry. When I got home, Mother was out collecting neighbourhood association fees, so I prepared dinner. We ate as soon as she got back. Then I wrote my diary, filled in my table of chores, wrote a letter to Father and went to bed.

Woke up: 7am **Went to bed:** 9pm **Study:** 1 hour **Chores:** prepared dinner

---

Collecting Fees

Japanese cities had to largely organise their own fire-fighting units, dig their own air-raid shelters and fortify their cities against firestorms. Voluntary neighbourhood associations had been set up in 1940, under the Imperial Rule Assistance laws, to oversee these home defence activities, and members had to take turns gathering fees from the neighbourhood to pay for them.

The associations were 'voluntary' in name only. In practice, social pressure and the *Kempeitai* – the military police – made sure everyone participated. Of course, many did so eagerly.

PH

19 May (Sat) Weather: rainy then cloudy, followed by more rain

School

Beautiful silken threads of rain are falling gently outside. I am writing my diary in silence, listening to the rain.

Today I was surprised to hear that Mizuiri Sensei has been sent to work at the prefectural office. Our new teacher will be Tsukiji Sensei. I will do as I am told and be a good girl in his class.

Home

I came home on the 5.47pm ferry. Mother had already returned from Hiroshima. After dinner, Mother and I talked about a lot of things. When I sat down at my desk later, many of the things that happened today came flooding back to me. I remembered that Tsukiji Sensei had learned music, just like Father did, and that made me miss Father, who is away fighting in the war, very much.

Woke up: 5.30am **Went to bed:** 9pm **Study:** 1 hour **Chores:** prepared dinner

Street Life

The silence Yoko notes in her entry of 19 May would have been temporary and unusual. In 1945, Hiroshima was full of life, despite the hardships of war. Sounds and smells were everywhere. On the parade ground at Hiroshima Castle you would hear orders being bellowed to troops. In the early morning, throughout the wards – or suburbs – you would hear the chants of family volunteers doing their morning exercises. In household shrines the people clapped awake the Shinto spirits. On street corners groups of workers awaited the trams, which came clanking down the tracks. And on demolition sites you could hear long lines of children like Yoko singing anti-American and anti-British slogans as they worked.

The city smelled horrible, because human excrement was used as fertiliser. The Japanese lacked any other kind. This 'night soil' was dumped in wagons every morning and taken to the inner-city vegetable gardens.

All over the city was the hue and cry of life struggling to feed itself, to live, and then every so often came the awful sound of the air-raid sirens, which most people now ignored.

PH

20 May (Sun) Weather: fine then cloudy

School

Today was a home training day.

Home

Today was a home training day and because I just rested from morning until evening, I feel as though something was somehow missing from my day. Even now as I write, a fierce battle is probably being fought in Okinawa. No, not 'probably'. It's really happening. We at home must also do our very best in everything we do.

Battle of Okinawa

Yoko and other children heard rumours of the dreadful battle fought on the remote Japanese island of Okinawa for eighty-two days, between April and June 1945. It was the first clash of arms between the Japanese and Americans on Japanese soil. The Americans needed the island as a 'jump-off' point for the aircraft and hundreds of thousands of troops expected to be used in a planned invasion later in the year.

The Americans were determined to capture the island, while the Japanese were ordered to fight to the death to defend it. The battle was the longest and worst of the Pacific War. More than 100,000 Japanese troops were killed, captured or committed suicide; and more than 70,000 Americans and Allied servicemen were killed or wounded. As well as this, tens of thousands of Okinawan civilians – who were terrified of falling into American hands after hearing false propaganda that they would be tortured – killed themselves by jumping off cliffs. The Japanese flew about 1500 *kamikaze* flights. Most crashed into the sea, but many slammed into the decks of US ships, sinking them. The people in Hiroshima knew none of the horrific details of the battle that came to be known in Japan as the 'Typhoon of Steel'.

PH

21 May (Mon) Weather: cloudy then rain

School

Today was another rainy day so I felt quite down in the dumps. When it rains, riding around on ferries and trains is a real bother.

We couldn't do our exercises today because of the rain, so we learned how to rub ourselves dry with wet towels instead. I am going to do this from now on.

Home

Because it looked as though it might rain today, I thought about taking an umbrella with me, but in the end I didn't. I was caught out though, because the rain started pelting down while I was on the way home. Next time I will definitely take an umbrella if it looks like it might rain.

Woke up: 5.20am **Went to bed:** 9pm **Study:** 1 hour **Chores:** prepared dinner

22 May (Tue) Weather: rain

School

A solemn ceremony was held at school today to commemorate the six-year anniversary of the Imperial Rescript for Young Students.

The deputy headmaster said, 'We must work hard because the fate of our country, Japan, rests on our shoulders.'

I am going to keep pressing on, no matter what.

Home

I was in the morning group today and it felt strange, just like it did when I joined the afternoon group. But it makes no difference whether we study in the morning or the afternoon. Either way, we must work hard. I am not going to give up.

Woke up: 5.20am **Went to bed:** 9pm **Study:** 1 hour **Chores:** prepared dinner

Imperial Rescript for Young Students

When Yoko refers to this in her diary, she probably means an updated version of Japan's Imperial Rescript on Education. A 'rescript' is a formal response by a government to a plea from the people. Rescripts were used as far back as Ancient Rome, when the emperors or consuls would issue them in reply to popular demands. In wartime Japan, the Imperial Rescript on Education – signed in 1890 during the Meiji era – was updated to directly address the mobilised students to encourage them to work harder. Perhaps the most famous rescript – which Yoko would have been aware of, since her father had recited it before he left to fight – was the Imperial Rescript to Soldiers and Sailors, issued by Emperor Meiji in January 1882. It urged all young men entering the armed forces to pledge absolute loyalty to the Emperor – to the death. Each man had to learn the rescript by heart. Its most famous line was: 'Duty is heavier than a mountain; death is lighter than a feather'.

PH

23 May (Wed) Weather: fine

School

Today we worked until ten o'clock clearing the evacuation route. After that, we cleaned the school kitchen. My hands were as black as soot after cleaning the stove, but I threw myself into the task anyway.

Home

I felt a little tired from doing physical labour and all that cleaning. But when I got home, I did a few things to help Mother and even ran an errand.

Woke up: 5.20am **Went to bed:** 9pm **Study:** 1 hour **Chores:** prepared dinner and ran an errand

24 May (Thu) Weather: fine

School

Today we put everything in order again after yesterday's great clean-up. As luck would have it, it was our job to tidy up the kitchen. I wiped the shelves and cleared the drain. I did my best because I was doing it for my country.

Home

Mother was sewing when I got home, so I did some things to help her. Then I read for a while, prepared for tomorrow's classes and revised what we learned at school today. After that, I helped prepare dinner. After we finished, I cleared everything away. I wrote my diary, filled in my table of chores and went to bed.

Woke up: 5.05am **Went to bed:** 9pm **Study:** 1 hour **Chores:** prepared dinner and did some sewing

---

25 May (Fri) Weather: fine

School

Today there was a ceremony to commemorate the day that Hirohito visited Kenjo in 1925, which was before he became Emperor. The headmaster read to us from a book written by the headmaster of that time, which contained his detailed reflections and recollections of that day. Two of the senior girls, Otsuji-san (Year 10) and Nakata-san (Year 8), also read us diary entries written by students of that time.

Home

When I got home we had a visitor from Iwakuni, so we talked about lots of things. I helped Mother to prepare dinner and the rations. Then I reviewed what we learned at school today, prepared for tomorrow's classes, wrote my diary and filled in my table of chores, before going to bed.

Woke up: 5.25am **Went to bed:** 9pm **Study:** 1 hour **Chores:** prepared dinner and rations

26 May (Sat) Weather: fine

School

I did labour service today. I was clearing the evacuation route as I normally do, but for some reason I felt very weak. But who cares about that compared to Father fighting in the war. Labour service has been called off [temporarily] as of today.

Home

When I got home, Mother wasn't there and that made me feel kind of lonely. After I had finished preparing dinner, I went to meet the 5.30pm ferry, which I thought she would take coming home. When the ferry pulled in and she was on it, for some reason it made me happy.

Woke up: 5.20am **Went to bed:** 9pm **Study:** 1 hour **Chores:** prepared dinner

27 May (Sun) Weather: fine

School

Today was a home training day and it was also Navy Day, the day when we commemorate the 1905 Battle of Tsushima.

Home

Because today was a home training day, Matsumoto-san from Hatsukaichi and Yamashita-san from Yawata had promised to visit me. For some reason, Yamashita-san did not end up coming over, but I had fun spending time and talking with Matsumoto-san.

Woke up: 6am **Went to bed:** 9pm **Study:** 1 hour **Chores:** prepared dinner

The Battle of Tsushima

Better known to us as the Sea of Japan Naval Battle, this battle was fought between Russia and Japan in May 1905 in the Tsushima Strait dividing Japan and Korea. Japan won. In fact, the Japanese fleet sank two-thirds of the Russian fleet. Their victory astonished the Western world. Until then, Britain and America had regarded Japan as an undeveloped country. Nobody dreamed that the Japanese could defeat the might of the Russian empire.

The Japanese won the Sea of Japan Naval Battle because of their superior technology. It was the first naval battle to be fought using wireless communication – that is, radio – between the ships. The Japanese wirelesses were far more effective than the Russian ones. Their first radio message sent by the Japanese naval commander to Tokyo said very confidently: 'I have just received news that the enemy fleet has been sighted. Our fleet will proceed forthwith to sea to attack the enemy and destroy him. Today's weather is fine but waves are high.'

Japan's great victories against Russia at Tsushima and Britain at Singapore were celebrated during the war, and girls like Yoko were taught to take pride in Japan's military strength.

PH

28 May (Mon) Weather: fine

School

From now on I will be in the afternoon group, so I caught the 10.40am ferry to school.

Because we live so far from school, I normally take a bento box with me for lunch and quickly eat it at school, in time to catch the early ferry home. But I am going to eat a little more slowly from now on.

Home

I came home on the 5.47pm ferry. Dinner was ready when I got home, so I ate straight away. Then I wrote my diary, filled in my table of chores and went to bed.

Woke up: 6am **Went to bed:** 9pm **Study:** 30 minutes **Chores:** cleared away after dinner

---

29 May (Tue) Weather: cloudy then fine

School

We had practical studies today, so we learned how to carry crates, plough fields and transport manure. Sasaki Sensei taught us for the first time in geography. Hori Sensei taught us how to draw graphs in mathematics.

Home

I came home on the 5.47pm ferry. As there was a little sticky rice left over, Mother had made some *kinako dango* rice dumplings. There weren't all that many of them, but I was delighted anyway. When I tried one I noticed it tasted a little salty but it was still delicious.

Woke up: 6am **Went to bed:** 9pm **Study:** 30 minutes **Chores:** prepared dinner

---

30 May (Wed) Weather: fine

School

We had household management class today, so we learned about teaching children proper etiquette. We need to remember that small children will get dirty learning how to feed themselves, but it is definitely a good idea not to help them.

Home

I had a slight toothache today, so I went straight to bed after dinner. Oh, I forgot to mention that my grandfather who lives in Yoshiwa came to see us today, so the whole house felt very festive and I was so happy to see him.

Woke up: 6am **Went to bed:** 9pm **Study:** 30 minutes **Chores:** cleared away after dinner

31 May (Thu) Weather: fine

School

My tooth was quite sore today, so I was feeling out of sorts with the world. It's hurting me so much now that I'm going to stop writing.

YOKO: Sensei, the senior girls cover their diaries in brightly coloured paper. May we do the same?
TSUKIJI SENSEI: Go right ahead.

Home

I got home and my tooth is still throbbing, so I'm not going to write any more now.

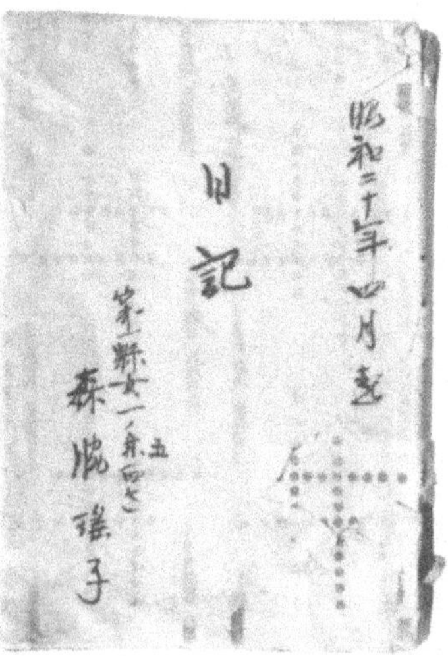

TSUKIJI SENSEI: When you have a toothache, you should get it treated as soon as possible. Go to the dentist.

Woke up: 6am **Went to bed:** 9pm **Study:** 30 minutes **Chores:** none

Yoko did cover her diary in bright paper. Later her mother wrote on its front: 'The diary of Yoko Moriwaki, a Year 7 student of Kenjo (Class B); April, 1945.' (Kohji Hosokawa)

June

1 June (Fri) Weather: fine then cloudy

School

Today was 1 June, so I visited the Gokoku Shrine for Fallen War Heroes. Looking up at the shrine gateway, I suddenly felt my body tense up with the solemnity of the place and I bowed down before the enshrined god and worshipped with all my heart.

I prayed that we would be ultimately victorious in the Greater East Asian War [Pacific War], that Father would have lasting good fortune in battle and that I would do a great job as class captain.

> TSUKIJI SENSEI: *The most important duty of a class captain is to act responsibly at all times. You must also be kind-hearted.*

Home

I was late for the 5.47pm ferry, which I normally take coming home, so I caught the 6.30pm ferry instead. Because of that I was ravenous. But who cares about that compared to Father and his comrades.

Yoko: Sensei, when I write with my fountain pen, the ink drips onto the page. What should I do?

Tsukiji Sensei: Dip the pen nib into the ink rather than pouring the ink into the pen and then try writing with it. Try to fix it. It's probably just loose.

Woke up: 5.30am **Went to bed:** 9pm **Study:** 1 hour **Chores:** prepared meals

2 June (Sat) Weather: fine

School

We were told that we would do labouring work today if the weather was fine, so I got everything ready for that before I left for school. But the sky suddenly clouded over, so labouring work was called off and we had classes instead. I felt so embarrassed because I didn't have my books. Next time I will look at the weather very carefully before I leave for school.

Home

On the way home I told the leader of my walking group that I wanted to visit my relatives in Teppocho, and she said I could go. I had an anxious moment on the way there when I got quite lost. I was so happy when I finally found my way again!

I came home on the 9.22pm ferry.

Woke up: 5.20am **Went to bed:** 10pm **Study:** 1 hour **Chores:** prepared dinner

Religion in Japan in the 1940s

Most Japanese families including Yoko's followed the national faith called Shinto. Followers were expected to worship their ancestors and pray to native spirits. During the war, Shinto belief was expressed in two ways. The first was state Shinto, which was the worship of the Imperial Way (that is, the Emperor). The second was folk or household Shinto, which was expressed in the daily practices that bound the ordinary Japanese people, such as praying at the family shrine, offering gifts to the spirits, traditional dancing, and purifying water and other cleansing rituals. Yoko's family were regular worshippers at the Shinto shrine in Miyajima, a practice called *omairi*. Yoko would stop before the gates, bow respectfully, wash her hands and feet, and clap twice to alert the spirits, then hold her hands in front of her chest.

Shinto was not the only religion practised in Japan. Many people also followed Buddhism, which came to Japan from China around the fifth century. Buddhism, unlike Shinto, offered the Japanese belief in an afterlife, namely reincarnation. Shinto tended to teach its followers how to behave in this life. Wartime Japan also had a very small Christian community, most of whom lived in Nagasaki and had done so for centuries, even though they were shunned and persecuted.

PH

3 June (Sun) Weather: fine

School

Today we worked clearing roads. I was in the morning group so it wasn't terribly hot, but I was sweating. But who cares about that compared to the battlefield.

I must do my best in everything until we win the war.

Home

I came home on the 2.20pm ferry. I was in the morning group so I got home earlier than usual. Our home looked old and familiar, as if I hadn't seen it in a long time. I suppose that's because I left so early this morning.

Woke up: 4.30am **Went to bed:** 9pm **Study:** 1 hour **Chores:** prepared dinner

Yoko's home in Miyajima. Hers is the house with the tree in the courtyard. (Kohji Hosokawa)

Japanese Homes

Japanese homes were made of paper. Well, not all of it was paper – really, a mixture of wood and specially treated paper. The rooms didn't have doors as our homes do. The doors were sliding doors made of wood and paper, called *fusuma*. The internal walls were in fact partitions that could be removed to create one big living space. Furniture was light and portable. Any room could become a 'living room', even the kitchen. In 1945, the ordinary Japanese heated their homes with charcoal – burnt wood – as coal was unobtainable by anyone other than the rich and powerful.

These were the traditional residences that packed the centre of Hiroshima and other cities. And they were extremely flammable. If one caught fire, the rest soon caught fire. No wonder most cities were reduced to ashes within hours of incendiary bombs falling.

PH

4 June (Mon) Weather: fine

School

Today we worked clearing roads again in the usual place.

The sun was beating down and I was sweating and felt exhausted, but then I looked at the road as it was gradually cleared and realised that it looked so much better than before, and that one always feels good after working hard.

Home

On the way home today, Fujita-san, who is one of the senior girls, told me she was going to buy oysters from Sakuma [a fishmonger in Miyajimaguchi], so I accompanied her because I had some time up my sleeve. Just as Sakuma came into view, Fujita-san suddenly realised that she had forgotten to bring something to put the oysters in, so we set off again to find a container.

Reflections

Today I had the tuberculosis vaccination and it hurt a lot. But I put on a brave face, as minor pain like that is nothing to complain about.

Woke up: 5.25am **Went to bed:** 9pm **Study:** 1 hour **Chores:** helped prepare dinner

---

5 June (Tues) Weather: fine

School

Today, right at this very moment, a fierce battle is being waged in Okinawa. I am sure that the British and American schoolgirls are working hard doing all sorts of things to win the war. We must not be outdone by those schoolgirls, we simply mustn't!

While I was studying today, a large number of enemy aircraft attacked the Kobe–Osaka region again. Schoolgirls like me may even have been hit by enemy fire and fallen like cherry blossom petals.

Fellow schoolgirls, you will surely be avenged. Rest in peace beneath the earth.

Home

Today I was delighted to arrive at the jetty in time for the 1.23pm ferry, which is very unusual for me. Then it occurred to me that right at the very moment I was feeling relieved because I was in time to catch the ferry, the planes of our bitter enemies were dropping bombs on the Japanese mainland. If enemy planes attack the mainland, it means that the mainland is a battlefield.

We are pushing forward on that battlefield, striving to increase production. If we will not work hard, who will? Whatever it takes, we must work as hard as we can until we win the war.

Woke up: 5.15am **Went to bed:** 8pm **Study:** 1 hour **Chores:** prepared dinner

---

The Imperial Japanese Army

Yoko often thinks of her father and the other soldiers fighting in the Pacific and at Okinawa. At the time, over five million men served in the Japanese Imperial Army: most were conscripts, meaning they were called up by the government and compelled to fight. Many volunteered, however. More than half of them were sent to China, Manchuria and other parts of the Japanese empire. By 1945 most were sick and hungry. Morale was low and supplies of food and ammunition were scarce. Huge numbers had been killed or wounded: more than 2.1 million Japanese servicemen would die by the end of the war, compared with around 417,000 US servicemen in both Europe and the Pacific and nearly 40,000 Australian servicemen in Europe and the Pacific.

The surviving Japanese soldiers could not get home to defend their country because the American naval blockade of Japan had shut them out. Left to defend the nation were the conscripted armed forces, the home guard and the Volunteer Fighting Corps, an army of civilians – many of them women and teenagers. The government in Tokyo ordered everyone – soldiers and civilians – to be prepared to fight to the death.

PH

6 June (Wed) Weather: fine

School

Today we learned household management from Sekiyama Sensei for the first time. Sekiyama Sensei is tall and kind. At the beginning of the lesson we did some revision before moving on to the next part.

I had my tuberculin reaction checked and it was positive. My scar is 1.4 centimetres long. [Yoko would have had a skin test to check whether she had been exposed to the bacteria that cause tuberculosis.]

Home

On the way home I had a word with my walking group leader and stopped by Grandmother's house. Grandmother was wearing reading glasses and using a hammer to do some carpentry. Mother had said she would come to Grandmother's house, so I waited for her, but she didn't come. I was really glad when she finally got there just when I was thinking about going home.

We came home on the 5.47pm ferry.

Woke up: 5.15am **Went to bed:** 10pm **Study:** 1 hour **Chores:** helped prepare dinner

7 June (Thu) Weather: fine

School

I had a slight toothache today but to my surprise it got better. I was so glad.

We were supposed to study physical science in our second lesson hour but Kurita Sensei was away so we did dressmaking instead. The warning siren sounded during the lesson, so we took cover in a bomb shelter straight away. Everyone was surprised because there was a frog in the bomb shelter. It caused quite a commotion.

Home

Today on the way home, I had a word with the leader of our walking group and went to see our relatives in Sendamachi. I waited for Mother again but she didn't come, so I felt lonely. But to my delight she finally came after I put on a brave face and waited a little longer.

Today is my birthday.

Woke up: 5.20am **Went to bed:** 9pm **Study:** 1 hour **Chores:** helped prepare dinner

8 June (Fri) Weather: fine

School

Today was Imperial Rescript Proclamation Day.

At school we flew the national flag, had a ceremony and listened to a reading of the Imperial Rescript on the Declaration of War. After that, our teacher checked how much cultivated land each of us has at home. I told him that Grandfather is very busy.

Home

Okayama-san, who was in my class when I was in Year 4 at national school, returned home from Hokkaido today. It was so good to see her again because she was my best friend. She has been attending Hokkaido Prefectural Girls' High School of Sapporo but will be coming to Kenjo from now on. I am going to pray that she passes the Kenjo school entrance exam.

Woke up: 5.20am **Went to bed:** 9pm **Study:** 1 hour **Chores:** helped prepare dinner

---

9 June (Sat) Weather: fine

School

Today our first lesson was biology and Kimura Sensei had everyone in stitches, as usual. At the beginning of his class, we put our hands together and say, 'Good morning.' But Kimura Sensei always makes us laugh by insisting that we say it too slowly. He is a really funny teacher!

Home

Today I rested for a while when I got home from school. Then, after eating, I spent some time with Okayama-san. Spending time with people can sometimes be boring, but when I'm with Okayama-san everything is kind of fun. We had such a great time visiting our old national school and saying hello to the teachers!

Woke up: 5.20am **Went to bed:** 8pm **Study:** 1 hour **Chores:** prepared dinner

10 June (Sun) Weather: fine

School

Today was a home training day.

Home

Today was a home training day. I had planned to sleep in, but my older brother, Kohji, is going to Kyushu on an errand for the Hiroshima Post and Telecommunications Bureau, so I helped to prepare various things for his trip.

It will be dangerous, so I prayed and asked God to keep Kohji safe.

Woke up: 5.20am **Went to bed:** 9pm **Study:** 1 hour **Chores:** prepared dinner

---

11 June (Mon) Weather: fine

School

Today we had labour service, so everybody gathered at Shijobashi Bridge before setting out for Hara Village. It was a long journey because Hara Village is so far away. When we got there, we visited the home of a family called the Matsumuras and helped them with some farm work. We had planned to cut wheat, but some students from Hiji Hill were already doing that so we helped in the fields instead.

Home

I was a little tired after doing labour service today but I gritted my teeth and just kept walking. On the way home, I stopped by Grandmother's house. Then I went home and helped Kohji prepare for his trip.

Woke up: 4am **Went to bed:** 11pm **Study:** 30 minutes **Chores:** prepared dinner

12 June (Tue) Weather: fine then cloudy

School

Today in our practical studies class we learned how to plant sweet potatoes. Munekuni Sensei told us that the only way to learn how to grow sweet potatoes really well is to actually do it – not just talk about it. He is right. I am going to take great care next time I grow sweet potatoes.

Home

Today Kohji left for his trip to Kyushu on the 9.28 train. It will be a dangerous trip. God, please protect my brother and keep him safe.

Woke up: 5.20am **Went to bed:** 9pm **Study:** 1 hour **Chores:** prepared dinner

---

13 June (Wed) Weather: rainy

School

Today we did dressmaking for four straight hours with Oka Sensei. I can scarcely contain my joy as I see my dress gradually starting to take shape. I hope it looks really lovely when it's finished!

Home

Yesterday I came home on the 6.32pm ferry but today I was lucky and got to the jetty in time to catch the 5.47pm ferry. I prepared for our national moral education class, wrote my diary and filled in my table of chores before going to bed.

Woke up: 6am **Went to bed:** 9pm **Study:** 1 hour **Chores:** prepared dinner

---

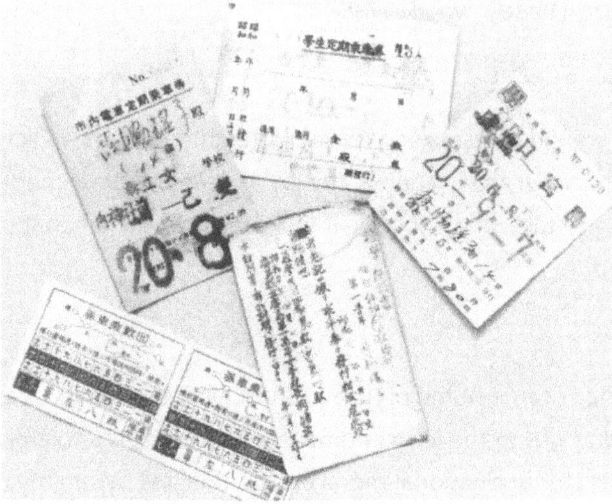

Top: *Various commuter passes Yoko used when she travelled to school.*
Bottom: *Yoko's purse, which she made herself. (Kohji Hosokawa)*

14 June (Thu) Weather: cloudy then fine

School

Today we went to work at Yoshijima Airport. We ploughed the fields and planted sweet potatoes and soy beans. While we were working, training fighter planes flew overhead performing marvellous, astonishing feats.

Home

My body felt a little weary today but I kept my chin up and came home on the 3.16pm ferry. I was quite bored when I got home because Mother wasn't there. But then I found a note on my desk from Mother. She wrote: 'I've gone to dig up pine roots. Don't go anywhere, I'll be back soon.' I felt much better after that and waited patiently for her to get home.

Woke up: 5.20am **Went to bed:** 9pm **Study:** 1 hour **Chores:** prepared dinner

15 June (Fri) Weather: rainy

School

Today we started making our summer uniforms. I cut out a piece of cloth and stitched the breast section. I felt happy but also amused by the whole thing, because I think we will look a bit strange. I couldn't help smiling when I imagined all of us travelling to school wearing uniforms made out of different coloured cloth but using the same pattern.

Home

Today was another gloomy, rainy day. How I hate the start of the monsoon when everything feels so damp! On the way home the train broke down and I had to change to another train at Itsukaichi. Because of that I was late for the 5.47pm ferry, so I was simply ravenous.

Woke up: 5.20am **Went to bed:** 9pm **Study:** 1 hour **Chores:** prepared dinner

---

16 June (Sat) Weather: fine

School

Today in our biology class we learned about beans. I was so embarrassed because I mixed up the spelling of two words that mean completely different things. They sound exactly the same but are spelt differently. I was really happy because we did dressmaking in our second and third lesson hours. In our fourth lesson hour we studied national literature and read a story called 'If I Had a Small Patch of Land'.

Home

I came home on the 5.47pm ferry. Dinner was ready when I got there, so I ate straight away.

When I sat down to write my diary there was a power blackout. The power suddenly came back on after a little while, but then it went out again just as I was about to start writing again. It was too bad!

Woke up: 6am **Went to bed:** 9pm **Study:** 1 hour **Chores:** cleared away after dinner

Power Blackouts

The lights went off – and on – every day in Japan during the later years of the war. The power supplies were very unreliable. The Japanese had very little coal and other fuels to power the generators. They had to ration energy as well as food. Coal, for example – which was critical for generating electricity – was virtually exhausted. So the people had to gather wood for use as fuel. When the electricity failed, they lit their homes with kerosene lamps powered by oil. The American naval blockade surrounding Japan was intended to destroy the Japanese economy and it succeeded.

PH

17 June (Sun) Weather: fine

School

Today was a home training day.

Home

Today I was very busy getting things ready because I will be doing farm work in Yoshiwa at my grandparents' farm tomorrow. I would like to take some small gifts to Yoshiwa to give to friends, but there are no such gifts during wartime. I suppose it's the thought that counts.

God, please protect us tomorrow so we get there safely.

Woke up: 6am **Went to bed:** 9pm **Study:** 1 hour **Chores:** cleared away after dinner

18 June (Mon) Weather: cloudy

School

Today I did farm work.

Home

This morning we left home early and went to buy tickets. The person in front of me in the queue bought the very last ticket, which was too bad, but I was glad to find out there was a truck that could take us there instead. We got to Yoshiwa at about 12 noon, and my grandparents were really happy to see us. I was quite tired today, so I didn't do much to help around the house.

Woke up: 5am **Went to bed:** 9pm **Study:** 30 minutes **Chores:** prepared dinner

19 June (Tue) Weather: fine

School

Today I did farm work.

Home

Today was my second day at Yoshiwa. My jobs are to wake up early in the morning and tend the chickens, prepare meals, clean up after meals, clean the house and pull up weeds outside the house and in the field. Then I rest for a while and start working again.

Woke up: 6am **Went to bed:** 9pm **Study:** 1 hour **Chores:** did farm work

20 June (Wed) Weather: fine with a shower then fine

School

Today I did farm work.

Home

When I awoke this morning, a lovely white fog was hanging over the plains and fields at the foot of the mountain. It was a splendid morning. Those chickens are so lovely – whenever I approach the chicken coop they start clucking because they are so happy to see me!

Woke up: 6am **Went to bed:** 9pm **Study:** 1 hour **Chores:** prepared meals

21 June (Thu) Weather: fine

School

Today I did farm work.

Home

Today was my third day at Yoshiwa. How time flies! Even though it feels like I just got here, I do sort of miss Kenjo and keep imagining my teachers' and friends' faces and the school grounds. Good old Kenjo – how I miss you!

Woke up: 6am **Went to bed:** 9pm **Study:** 1 hour **Chores:** prepared meals

22 June (Fri) Weather: fine with intermittent showers in the evening

School

Today I did farm work.

Home

Today I took care of my relative Mineko. Her mother is staying at Amano Hospital in Tsuda at the moment because she is ill. Even though Mineko is only two years old, she isn't fussing because she misses her mother. She is being a good girl and just waiting patiently.

Woke up: 5am **Went to bed:** 9pm **Study:** 1 hour **Chores:** prepared meals

23 June (Sat) Weather: rainy

School

Today I did farm work.

Home

Today was windy and it poured with rain. It actually felt quite cold. Grandmother planted rice and Grandfather tilled the fields with his cattle-drawn plough.

Woke up: 6am **Went to bed:** 9pm **Study:** 1 hour **Chores:** prepared meals

24 June (Sun) Weather: fine with intermittent showers in the evening

School

Today I did farm work, and it was a home training day.

Home

Today for the first time ever I planted rice. It was awful as my feet kept sinking deep down into the oozy mud. But who cares about that, compared to the benefit that this rice will be to our country?

The rice we are cultivating will be distributed to people all over Japan. With that thought firmly in my mind, I put everything I had into the job at hand.

Woke up: 6am **Went to bed:** 9pm **Study:** 1 hour **Chores:** prepared meals

---

25 June (Mon) Weather: fine

School

Today I did farm work.

Home

Mother set out at about 6am this morning to walk home to Miyajima, so I felt sort of lonely today. She will get back to Yoshiwa on about the twenty-ninth, so I will have to wait about four days before I see her again. I hope she comes back soon!

Mother, come back soon!

Woke up: 5.30am **Went to bed:** 9pm **Study:** 1 hour **Chores:** prepared meals

26 June (Tue) Weather: fine

School

Today I did farm work.

Home

I felt sort of lonely again today. I hope Mother comes back soon; it's on my mind day and night. I keep reminding myself that many children younger than me have been separated from their parents and evacuated to the countryside, but then I just start feeling lonely again.

Woke up: 6am **Went to bed:** 9pm **Study:** 1 hour **Chores:** prepared meals

27 June (Wed) Weather: fine with intermittent showers in the evening

School

Today I did farm work.

Home

Mother is finally coming back either tomorrow or the day after and I just can't wait to see her again! Grandmother and Grandfather dote on me fondly, but of course Mother is the one I love most of all.

I've heard that Yoshiwa has a tradition called Dorootoshi, which celebrates the end of rice planting on 30 June. Everyone will take a one-day holiday.

Woke up: 6am **Went to bed:** 9pm **Study:** 1 hour **Chores:** did farm work

---

28 June (Thu) Weather: fine

School

Today I did farm work.

Home

I hoped that Mother would come back today and waited for her, but she never came. She will definitely come back tomorrow and I'm really looking forward to seeing her. It feels like the last time I saw her was so long ago. I can't wait for tomorrow to come!

Woke up: 6am **Went to bed:** 9pm **Study:** 1 hour **Chores:** prepared meals

29 June (Fri) Weather: rainy

School

Today I did farm work.

Home

I am beside myself with worry because Mother was supposed to come back today and she didn't. Why, oh why, didn't she come? She promised she would be here on the twenty-ninth. I was so happy and excited today because I was sure she would come back. Now I'm lonely all over again.

Woke up: 6am **Went to bed:** 9pm **Study:** 1 hour **Chores:** prepared meals

30 June (Sat) Weather: Rainy then fine

School

Today I did farm work.

Home

I waited for Mother to finally arrive today. The regular bus service comes every other day, so it was supposed to come today. The bus arrived at lunch time. Just as I was thinking, 'She's actually here!' Mother appeared. I was so happy to see her.

Woke up: 6am **Went to bed:** 9pm **Study:** 1 hour **Chores:** prepared meals

Yoko and her mother in 1944. (Kohji Hosokawa)

July

1 July (Sun) Weather: rainy

School

Today I did farm work.

Home

Woke up: 6am **Went to bed:** 9pm **Study:** 1 hour **Chores:** prepared meals, planted sweet potato

It rained today, so Grandfather and I put on our straw rain gear and planted sweet potatoes. The rain had eased off slightly when we finished, so I pulled up weeds in the garden with a friend.

2 July (Mon) Weather: fine

School

Today I did farm work.

Home

Today was a simply glorious day – totally unlike the weather we have had recently.

It was calm and not too hot, with a pleasant breeze. It was the kind of day that reminds you of spring. The day after tomorrow I will go home to Miyajima. I'm so looking forward to seeing my teachers and friends again – it's been ages since I last saw them!

Woke up: 6am **Went to bed:** 9pm **Study:** 1 hour **Chores:** prepared meals

---

3 July (Tue) Weather: fine

School

Today I did farm work.

Home

I have mixed feelings about finally going home tomorrow. I do miss Miyajima but at the same time I don't want to leave Yoshiwa. As I sign off here today, I'm hoping against hope that there will be a bus or a truck tomorrow.

Woke up: 6am **Went to bed:** 9pm **Study:** 1 hour **Chores:** prepared meals

4 July (Wed) Weather: fine

School

Today I did farm work.

Home

I heard that a truck would leave between nine and ten o'clock this morning, so I quickly got ready and waited out the front of the Union building. It arrived at 8.30am. I got on, changed to a bus for Hatsukaichi at Tsuda and caught the 5.47pm ferry back home from Miyajimaguchi.

Woke up: 6am **Went to bed:** 9pm **Study:** none **Chores:** prepared dinner

5 July (Thu) Weather: fine

School

I was too tired to go to school today so I rested at home.

Home

I didn't go to school today because I was so tired from all the farm work I have been doing right up to yesterday. There is a holiday until the seventh for the farmers' busy season, but when I told Mother I would go to school she told me that I would end up having to rest at home for a long time if I went out when I was tired. So I decided to stay home instead.

Woke up: 6am **Went to bed:** 9pm **Study:** 1 hour **Chores:** prepared dinner

6 July (Fri) Weather: fine with evening showers then cloudy

School

Today we marched to Yagi Training Hall to put valuables belonging to the school in safe storage. The books that I was given weren't all that heavy, but by the time I got halfway there I didn't care how light they were, I simply wanted to throw them away! I did my best though.

Home

I caught the 6.30pm ferry home. When I got home, Mother was waiting for me and making dinner, which tasted wonderful because I was absolutely famished!

Even I was impressed that I walked 25 kilometres today. To think that I will be able to walk really long distances from now on – even 25 kilometres!

Woke up: 5.20am **Went to bed:** 9pm **Study:** 30 minutes **Chores:** prepared dinner

7 July (Sat) Weather: fine

School

Yesterday I walked over 25 kilometres, so my legs are a little sore. But who cares about that compared to all the marching our soldiers do.

We cleaned in the first lesson hour. Then, just when we thought we had finished, the warning siren sounded, so we all lined up and the students who live outside the city took the school's books home to keep in safe storage.

Home

Just as the train was about to pull into the terminal, the ferry pulled away from the jetty. It was too bad! Because the 11am ferry had left, I had to wait for about one hour and fifteen minutes – until 12.15pm – to catch the next ferry.

When Oka-san and I suggested that we eat lunch, Fujita-san, who is a senior girl, told us to go ahead and eat. So we did.

Woke up: 5.20am **Went to bed:** 11pm **Study:** 1 hour **Chores:** prepared dinner

---

8 July (Sun) Weather: fine

School

Today was a home training day.

Home

Today was a home training day. My grandparents sent us some charcoal from their home in the countryside, so we went to Hatsukaichi last night to collect it. Because I went to bed at about 11pm, I felt sort of sleepy today.

But Japan is fighting a war, so it doesn't matter how sleepy I feel – I must do my best at all times.

TSUKIJI SENSEI: *I'm proud of you for all the hard work you did helping your grandparents on the farm. But you seem to have fallen slightly behind with your studies, so make sure you work hard from now on.*

Woke up: 6am **Went to bed:** 11pm **Study:** 1 hour **Chores:** prepared meals

---

9 July (Mon) Weather: fine

School

Today Yoshimura Sensei gave us a lecture about incendiary bombs and showed us an empty oil bomb. He told us that incendiary bombs are not really all that scary, because if they are extinguished quickly there is nothing to worry about.

I think he's right.

Home

Today, Tsukiji Sensei taught us how to make a substitute for rice or wheat. First you steam potato over a bed of rice. Then you mush up the potato, fry it with a little oil, put some yellow pickled radish or vegetables in the centre, and then roll it up just like sushi. Next time we get potato, I am going to try making it.

Woke up: 5.20am **Went to bed:** 9pm **Study:** 1 hour **Chores:** prepared dinner

---

False Hope

The firebombing raids that had been occurring in Japan went on for five months, and by the end of July about sixty-six Japanese cities were in smoking ruins. The people of Hiroshima expected that they would suffer the same fate, but it never came. The reason? Hiroshima was being preserved. The American commanders had marked it, along with four other Japanese cities, as a target for the nuclear bomb. To bomb it beforehand would not show the devastating power of the new atomic weapon to best effect. As Winston Churchill, the British Prime Minister said, it would simply 'make the rubble dance'.

It seemed strange to the people of Hiroshima that their city had not been the target of US aircraft. The people had heard rumours that the Americans were going to spare their city. In Nagasaki, where the second atomic bomb was dropped on 9 August, the people wondered if their city was being spared because of their large Christian community. The truth was cruel.

PH

10 July (Tue) Weather: fine then cloudy

School

Today in our fifth lesson hour we were told what each walking group should do if our school or homes burn down. If that happens we are to meet at Koi National School.

Home

I had dinner as soon as I got home today and then started working on my household management homework, which was to make a toy for a small child to carry or play with using natural materials. I made a bag that hangs from the waist.

Woke up: 5.20am **Went to bed:** 9pm **Study:** 1 hour **Chores:** cleared away after dinner

---

11 July (Wed) Weather: cloudy then rainy

School

Today the headmaster did not come to our national moral education class, so Sasaki Sensei took the class instead. Our name tags are going to change. 'Kenjo' will be printed horizontally in the upper 2-centimetre section of a white 8-centimetre-long by 3-centimetre-wide piece of cloth, and our name and blood type will be printed vertically in the lower section.

Home

The warning siren sounded just as I finished eating the food in my bento box, so I came straight home on the 2.20pm ferry. Then I made some dolls out of wool. I prepared for tomorrow's classes and went to bed.

Woke up: 5am **Went to bed:** 9pm **Study:** 1 hour **Chores:** prepared dinner

---

12 July (Thu) Weather: rainy

School

The train was late today, so our first lesson had already started when I got to school. In biology class, Kimura Sensei read us a letter he had received from Hiroshima Prefectural Kure Girls' High School. Apparently, their most important job is putting clothes in safe storage.

Home

I came home on the 12.15pm ferry. After I finished studying, I played a game with my friend Oka-san. It was great fun even though it was just the two of us.

Woke up: 5.30am **Went to bed:** 9pm **Study:** 1 hour **Chores:** prepared dinner

---

13 July (Fri) Weather: fine

School

Water had collected in the bomb shelters so we scooped it up and poured it away. I used a bucket to bail out the water in bomb shelter number one. It was not an easy job but I did my best. I was tired but felt great when it was all finished!

Home

Although we were supposed to study until our fifth lesson hour today, lessons were suspended until lunchtime, so I did some cleaning and then came home on the 2.20pm ferry.

Woke up: 5.20am **Went to bed:** 9pm **Study:** 1 hour **Chores:** prepared dinner

14 July (Sat) Weather: cloudy

School

On 1 May we farewelled the Year 10 girls who have been sent to the manufacturing battlefront. Next, we will farewell the Year 8 girls. One hundred girls will be sent to the Hiroshima Printing Company, another hundred to a school factory in Kouchi Village which produces military supplies, and sixty to Hiroshima Air Base. Most of them will be mobilised on the eighteenth. They will be just like our brave soldiers.

Now we Year 7 students are the only ones left, so we must do our best at all times.

Home

Tomorrow is a special home training day, so we planned to go swimming at Nagahama Beach with the Year 8 students who live in Kusatsu and Itsukaichi. But as luck would have it, it is pouring with rain right now; really awful rain. I wish it would hurry up and stop raining!

Woke up: 5.20am **Went to bed:** 9pm **Study:** 1 hour **Chores:** prepared dinner

---

15 July (Sun) Weather: fine

School

Today was a home training day.

Home

It rained last night, so I woke up expecting that today would be a disappointing day. But to my surprise and delight the weather outside was glorious!

When I went out to meet the 9.47am ferry, everyone was already there. We all headed to Nagahama together and had great fun swimming there. After that, we all returned home on the 3.30pm ferry.

Woke up: 6am **Went to bed:** 9pm **Study:** 1 hour **Chores:** prepared dinner

---

16 July (Mon) Weather: fine then cloudy with occasional showers

School

Today in our first lesson hour Tsukiji Sensei taught us how to use a triangular bandage to wrap the head, ears, eyes and chin. I was on tenterhooks because I thought that we might have a history test, but to my relief we didn't.

Home

The warning siren sounded today, so I came home on the 2.20pm ferry. By the time I did my homework, revision and prepared for tomorrow's classes, it was 5pm. So I had dinner, wrote my diary and went to bed.

Woke up: 5.20am **Went to bed:** 9pm **Study:** 2 hours **Chores:** prepared dinner

17 July (Tue) Weather: rainy

School

Today the Year 8 students were finally mobilised to work in military supply factories. We Year 7 students stood at the school gate and clapped as they left. I nearly started crying.

All of a sudden I felt lonely, as it occurred to me that from today we Year 7 students will be the only ones left at school. But I decided that this means we must do a great job holding the fort while everyone else is away.

Home

I came home on the 3.16pm ferry. Today's household management homework was to tidy just one room by myself and to make a note of the size of that room and the order in which each cleaning task was performed. So I tidied my study room and measured its dimensions.

Woke up: 5.30am **Went to bed:** 9pm **Study:** 1 hour **Chores:** prepared dinner

18 July (Wed) Weather: fine

School

Today I noticed that because only the Year 7 students are left, the playground seems strangely bigger than before. Because the Year 8 students are gone, we also have more cleaning duties. We must do an even better job from now on.

Home

The warning siren sounded at the end of our fourth lesson hour, so I left school straight away and came home on the 2.20pm ferry. Mother went to Hiroshima today so I felt sort of drained when I got home.

This pen has a large nib and leaks. The nib of my last pen broke.

Woke up: 4.30am **Went to bed:** 10pm **Study:** 1 hour **Chores:** prepared dinner

19 July (Thu) Weather: fine

School

Mother left home early today, so we caught the 5.20am ferry to school together. It made me realise that I far prefer leaving home early in the morning and arriving at school early to leaving home late and arriving at school late.

Home

I finished lunch and headed to the public health centre to have my blood type checked, but the warning siren sounded the very moment I passed out of the school gate. It was too bad! So I came home on the 2.20pm ferry.

Woke up: 4.30am **Went to bed:** 10pm **Study:** 1 hour **Chores:** prepared dinner

---

20 July (Fri) Weather: cloudy with occasional rain

Today I heard that we will all be moved to different classes tomorrow. It is sad to think that we will be split up, having become such good friends. But Japan is at war and so I know that now is not the time to fret about small things. No matter how lonely I am, I must keep my spirits up and work hard.

Home

I took the 4.02pm ferry home. Today we ate peaches and green peas, which were absolutely delicious. But then I remembered Father fighting in the war and felt guilty knowing that he and his comrades probably wouldn't have anything as delicious to eat as the meal I had just enjoyed.

Woke up: 5am **Went to bed:** 9.30pm **Study:** 1 hour **Chores:** prepared dinner

21 July (Sat) Weather: rainy then fine

Today in our first lesson hour we were all moved to different classes. Even though I felt really sad parting with my new friends, I bade them farewell cheerfully.

Then at 9.30am I headed to the public health centre to have my blood type checked. It hurt a little but I found out that I am type A.

Home

On the way home, I stopped by the house of my grandmother who lives in Takasu. I was glad I went to see her, because she was so happy to see me. I took the 6.30pm ferry home.

Woke up: 5.20am **Went to bed:** 9pm **Study:** 1 hour **Chores:** prepared dinner

22 July (Sun) Weather: fine

School

Today was a home training day.

Home

I woke up early this morning but went to bed again because I had a headache and 39.5-degree fever.

Woke up: 5.30am **Went to bed:** 6pm **Study:** none **Chores:** none

23 July (Mon) Weather: fine

School

I didn't go to school today because I had a fever.

Home

I really wanted to go to school today but I couldn't because I had a fever.

Woke up: 6am **Went to bed:** 8pm **Study:** none **Chores:** none

24 July (Tue) Weather: fine

School

I didn't go to school today because there was an air raid. The warning siren didn't go off until 10am. Then it started again in the afternoon and continued for quite a long time.

Home

An air raid started when I got on the ferry this morning, so the ferry was cancelled. I went home and waited for the warning siren to go off. When it finally went off and I decided to go to school, the air raid started again. The warning siren didn't go off until ten so I didn't go to school today.

It makes me so mad to think that the enemy prevented us from having classes, even if it was just for one day!

Woke up: 5.20am **Went to bed:** 9pm **Study:** 1 hour **Chores:** prepared dinner

---

25 July (Wed) Weather: fine

School

I didn't go to school today because, just like yesterday, there was an air raid.

Home

I couldn't go to school today because, of course, just like yesterday, there was an air raid. Today was the day of the Itsukushima Shrine Kangensai Festival. It is usually a very lively festival, but this year it wasn't lively at all. It was just a lonely, lonely festival with no street stalls.

Woke up: 5.25am **Went to bed:** 9pm **Study:** 1 hour **Chores:** prepared dinner

---

Itsukushima Shrine Kangensai Festival

Every year, Miyajima Island holds a beautiful music festival, featuring a waterborne stage formed out of boats. The boats are draped in colourful curtains and linked with lanterns. It is a ceremony on the sea. The audience watches aboard their own boats or from the shore. The performances climax at midnight with the return of the boats to shore, including one carrying the deity of the shrine. Up until the end of the war, the festival was held in July. It is now held in August. The festival dates back to the Heian era (eighth to twelfth century), and celebrates the deity of the shrine.

In Yoko's time, the ceremony was much the same as today. Local musicians performed on traditional Japanese instruments – flutes, stringed instruments and drums. One boat staged traditional Japanese Noh theatre. Yet there was one big difference. Instead of food and shopping stalls offering a feast of local produce, in 1945 there was virtually no food for sale – just rice and potatoes. That year the Kangensai Festival was a drab affair. It would have been a sad reminder to Yoko of the war all around her.

PH

26 July (Thu) Weather: cloudy with a little rain then fine

School

Today we had a physical science test. We had to write about something we would like to conduct an experiment on, so I wrote about lightshades.

Home

On the way home, I visited my grandmother who lives in Takasu, and by coincidence I ran into my older brother, Kohji, at the ferry terminal. He has returned from Kyushu, so he came to our house. I am so happy because he will be commuting to the Hiroshima Post and Telecommunications Bureau from our house, so things will be quite lively at home from now on.

Woke up: 5.10am **Went to bed:** 10pm **Study:** 1 hour 30 minutes **Chores:** prepared dinner

27 July (Fri) Weather: fine

School

Today we had a music lesson with Nagahashi Sensei. We practised singing songs. It was fun, just like Tsukiji Sensei's classes. I heard that Nagahashi Sensei also taught my mother when she was a student at Yamanaka Girls' High School. I never imagined that Nagahashi Sensei was so old!

Home

Today, I visited my grandmother who lives in Takasu again. Kohji bought fish yesterday, so I invited her to our house for dinner.

Things are quite lively at home now because we have one more person staying with us. I'm so happy!

Woke up: 5.15am **Went to bed:** 9.30pm **Study:** 1 hour **Chores:** prepared dinner

28 July (Sat) Weather: fine

School

I couldn't go to school today because there was an air raid.

Home

Today, just like on the twenty-fourth and twenty-fifth, some small airplanes attacked Hiroshima. It was so scary watching those horrid airplanes fly over Miyajima.

Woke up: 5.15am **Went to bed:** 9.30pm **Study:** 1 hour **Chores:** prepared dinner

---

29 July (Sun) Weather: fine then cloudy

School

Today was a home training day.

Home

Today I visited my relatives living in Inokuchi. After I had walked for quite a while my legs felt unbearably tired. They gave me some peaches, so I brought them home.

Woke up: 6am **Went to bed:** 9.30pm **Study:** 1 hour 30 minutes **Chores:** prepared dinner

---

30 July (Mon) Weather: cloudy then fine then cloudy again

School

Today I went to school but an air-raid siren sounded just as we were having morning assembly, so we all went home. When I reached Koi, the siren went off so I went back to school and had classes.

Today we farewelled Nishino Sensei and Tsuji Sensei.

Home

I came home on the 3.16pm ferry. I was terribly thirsty, so as soon as the ferry docked I raced home and drank some water. It tasted wonderful!

Woke up: 5.15am **Went to bed:** 9.30pm **Study:** 1 hour **Chores:** prepared dinner

31 July (Tue) Weather: cloudy

School

I stayed at school late and did dressmaking today because I fell behind making my summer uniform while I was away doing farm work in Yoshiwa. I was glad that I had only a small amount left to do. It is finally finished!

Today, Yoko Nishino left to attend a school in Yamaguchi Prefecture. I feel sad because I will miss her. Take care, Nishino-san!

Home

Because I stayed at school until late, I got to the ferry terminal later than usual and caught the 6.32pm ferry home.

Everyone was waiting for me when I arrived, and we all had fun eating dinner together.

But my heart goes out to the people of Tokyo, where so many have lost parents or children and are now all alone.

Woke up: 5.10am **Went to bed:** 9.30pm **Study:** 1 hour **Chores:** prepared dinner

---

August

1 August (Wed) Weather: cloudy

School

Today it suddenly struck me: 'It's 1 August. Summer is really here now.' As it was the first day of the month, I visited the Gokoku Shrine for Fallen War Heroes. After that, I was in a much better mood and felt refreshed and clear-headed.

Home

I'm so happy that my work trousers are finished. I'm so happy I simply can't say the words 'I'm happy' enough! We are going to sew some gym clothes next, and I'm going to be careful not to fall behind this time.

Woke up: 4.30am **Went to bed:** 10.30pm **Study:** 1 hour 30 minutes **Chores:** prepared dinner

---

2 August (Thu) Weather: cloudy

School

I felt very ashamed today because I was late to school, even though Tsukiji Sensei had a word with me yesterday about being late.

I caught the suburban train early so that I would get to school on time but I couldn't get on a city train. All the way there I was thinking, 'I must hurry!' but I ended up being late anyway.

Home

Woke up: 4.50am **Went to bed:** 9.30pm **Study:** 1 hour 30 minutes **Chores:** prepared dinner

---

Today as I wrote my diary I remembered the diaries Tsukiji Sensei read to us. They were reflective in tone and beautifully written. I would really like to be able to write like that, so I will keep trying.

3 August (Fri) Weather: fine

School

Today we visited the Kenjo agricultural plot in Takeyacho. The plot hadn't been very well tended, so a lot of grass had grown up. Everyone worked hard to remove the grass, so the black soil was gleaming in next to no time. Then we turned the soil over again and ploughed most of it.

It was hot, sweaty work, but I felt really good after I had finished.

Home

Woke up: 4.40am **Went to bed:** 10pm **Study:** 1 hour **Chores:** prepared dinner

Today I felt a little tired but who cares about that. The senior girls are working so hard in places all over Hiroshima, so how can I complain about being tired? We are going to the agricultural plot again tomorrow and I am going to work hard.

4 August (Sat) Weather: fine

School

Today we worked at the agricultural plot again. It was just as hot as yesterday but I put up with the heat and worked as hard as I could.

Home

On the way home, the wind blew my hat into the sea at the jetty. It hovered before my eyes for a brief moment but I couldn't catch it. When I think of Mother going to all the trouble of buying that hat for me ... it is just too bad! I am really upset about it.

Woke up: 5am **Went to bed:** 9.30pm **Study:** 1 hour **Chores:** prepared dinner

5 August (Sun) Weather: fine

School

Today was a home training day.

Home

Today was the day of working at home. Yesterday my uncle came and so the house was very lively. I wish every day would be like that.

From tomorrow morning we are joining the home demolition groups. I am going to do my best.

Woke up: 6am **Went to bed:** 9pm **Study:** 1 hour 30 minutes **Chores:** prepared meals

This day marks the end of Yoko's diary. On 6 August, Yoko bore the full brunt of the atomic bomb blast when she was working outdoors in the Dobashi area, about 700 metres from the hypocentre. That evening, she died in a relief centre, 10 kilometres away.

Our father, Ataru Moriwaki, learned of Yoko's death the following year after he was repatriated from China. Years later, in place of his daughter, he wrote the following entry in Yoko's diary for 6 August.

– Kohji Hosokawa

6 August (Mon) Weather: fine

Sweet Yoko,
Father lost the war and came home to find you gone. I miss you terribly, so I am going to write the final entry in the diary you kept each day while you waited for me to return.

Full of a sense of your responsibilities as class captain, you set out on the first ferry of the day to do labour service demolishing houses in the Dobashi area, so that Japan could win the war.

At 8.15 in the morning, you bore the full brunt of that terrible atomic blast. Covered in severe burns, you were carried to Kannon Village National School in Saeki District, with your teacher, Mitsuya Sensei.

You waited anxiously for Mother and Father to arrive but we never came. Finally, you drew your last lonely breath at 11.24 that evening, uttering the words, 'Isn't Mother here yet?' You were all alone.

The one small comfort you enjoyed was the tender care of Dr Awase and Hatsue Ueda, who nursed you.

Yoko, may your spirit rest in peace.

Mother and I sing this song which I wrote while thinking of you as I waited at an internment facility in Shanghai for the repatriation boat. We dedicate it to you, our beloved daughter, who is waiting for us far away.

Beloved Daughter

1.

In Momijidani Park of the island I know well
Your sweet eyes once danced to see the deer.
In the two years you and Mother were alone
You played the melodies I taught you
Softly striking the keys with your fingers.

2.

In the lonely land where Father lives
At the other side of this long stretch of time
Winds buffet my temporary home
Bearing news that darkens the night
And the frosts chill even my bitterness.

3.

A terrible nightmare it has been
My spirit, once tested, is now glad.
On a morning free from the horrors of war
I talk with a friend, gazing at the eastern sky
And tears burn my eyes.

When he returned home bearing this song as a gift, our father discovered that Yoko, who should have been there waiting for him, had been killed in the atomic bomb blast. Although it was originally a cheerful melody composed in a major key, Father rewrote the melody in a minor key, and thus it became a sad song that mourned his daughter's death. Both the sheet music and the lyrics shown here were composed by our father.

– Kohji Hosokawa

「娘いとし」

一、懐かしの島紅葉谷（もみじだに）
鹿と戯むる愛（いと）しき瞳
母と二人の二年（ふたとせ）を
父が奏（かな）でしメロディを
やさしき指に弾きつらん

二、愁（かな）しくも父大陸の
永き流れのその果ての
仮のやどりにしのぐ風
便りを乗せて吹ける夜
恨みもさめて霜寒し

三、恐ろしき夜夢の夢
霊（たま）の験（ためし）の幸の辺に
戦（いくさ）の災（わざわい）なき朝は
友と語りて東（ひんがし）の
空を仰げば眼も熱し

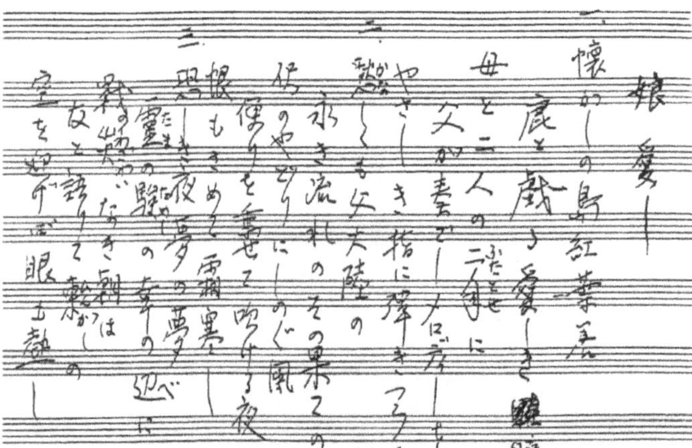

父が 1946 年 2 月 23 日、上海で作った「娘愛し」の歌詞と楽譜（次ページ）

Japanese lyrics to the song 'Beloved Daughter'.

Sheet music for the song 'Beloved Daughter', which Yoko's father composed in Shanghai on 23 February 1946.

Tribute
from a brother

The letter from Hatsue Ueda

Immediately after the atomic bomb was dropped on 6 August 1945, hospitals, schools and other facilities located in the suburbs of Hiroshima became emergency relief centres. One after another, the injured were carried to those relief centres in military trucks or boats.

Amidst all the chaos, Yoko, who was critically injured, was lifted into a relief truck and taken from atomic-bombed Dobashi to a relief centre located approximately 10 kilometres away in the science laboratory of the Kannon Village National School in Saeki District, Hiroshima Prefecture; she was admitted at around noon.

A young local housewife called Hatsue Ueda nursed Yoko and attended her deathbed in the last hours of her life.

While she was taking care of my sister, Mrs Ueda tried to contact Mother in Miyajima several times. However, in all the chaos, she was unable to reach her. Meanwhile, Mother spent a sleepless night at home and then the next day, on the seventh, hurried to the relief centre after word finally reached us from the village office.

For her part, Yoko waited anxiously for Mother and breathed her last, lonely breath that night, clinging to Mrs Ueda's hand and calling out for our mother.

At the sight of Yoko's lifeless corpse, Mother suffered the deepest sorrow imaginable and was prostrate with grief.

Mrs Ueda, who had experienced something most people would never imagine in their worst nightmares, described Yoko's condition and last moments in a letter she wrote to Michiko Kigami, a friend who lived in Miyajima, the same small island where Yoko lived.

Later that year, Ms Kigami sent us the letter. Mother cried and cried when she read it. For the rest of us who no longer cry, the letter is a reminder of our profound grief.

7 August 1945

Dear Michiko,

Yesterday was a terrible day in Hiroshima. I know it is strange that I am suddenly writing to you now. I trust you were not injured? I pray that you somehow managed to escape and returned home safely. We have all been terribly concerned about you.

I hope that your family in Miyajima was unharmed.

How are your dear father, mother, aunt and grandmother? I trust they are all still doing well. All of you are in my thoughts.

We, thank heavens, were all unharmed, so please don't worry about us. Our shoji screens and other things inside our home were destroyed, so we escaped with only our lives. My younger brother and sister had been permitted to rest at home, as they were rather unwell, which turned out to be a blessing in disguise.

Right now, there are about 150 people at Kannon School. I went there to do relief work yesterday evening. All members of the women's and young women's associations have been mobilised. At the relief station I came across a person who said she was from Miyajima. When she told me where she was from, I felt very attached to her and nursed her injuries so that I didn't have to leave her side.

She was very badly injured; her whole body was covered in severe burns and it was obvious that she couldn't be saved, so I just did everything I could for her. She just stared at the clock, waiting anxiously for her mother to come and see her. I had someone at the village office telephone her home in Miyajima, so we waited and waited for her mother to come, wondering whether or not she had arrived yet.

I don't know how many times she asked me, 'Isn't Mother here yet?' and I comforted her by saying, 'She'll be here soon. Be strong and stay with me, okay?'

When she asked me to give her water or green tea, or stroke her back, or rub her chest, or drum lightly on her chest, or hold her hand, or fan her because she felt hot, I did as she asked and held her hand in mine.

I waited like that with her for her mother to arrive, but in the end, she died before her mother could get there.

She died while the doctor was taking her pulse.

I simply have no words to express how sad it was.

That poor, poor, poor girl!

Then, while I was caring for her, it occurred to me that you might also be out there somewhere, injured, like her, and I couldn't stop worrying. When you get home safely, please contact me immediately as I am very concerned.

Apparently, the girl who passed away was Yoko Moriwaki (thirteen years old), a Year 7 student from Kenjo. She had been in the Dobashi area doing labour service. While the doctor was taking her pulse, he said, 'I've heard that this girl is the music teacher's daughter.' When I asked her if she knew you, she told me very clearly that she did. I asked her if she lived near you, and she said, 'Yes.'

You must know her well too.

Her mother must be grieving and terribly distraught that she arrived too late. The girl wasn't even wearing her school uniform because it had been burnt right off her body.

If you do see anyone from her family, please let them know that although the facility was rudimentary and the nursing treatment only basic, she received the very warmest care from everybody. We did the very best we could to enable her to pass away peacefully.

She died at 11.24pm on 6 August.

My dear Michiko, please contact me with news. I am anxiously waiting to hear from you.

Please give my regards to your parents, your grandmother and your aunt.

Yours,

Hatsue Ueda

Present-day Dobashi, the area where Yoko and her classmates were doing labour service when the atomic bomb was dropped on Hiroshima. (Kohji Hosokawa)

Yoko, rest in peace

With each year that passed after the war, things gradually settled and returned to normal, and Japanese people found themselves living in a new peaceful, prosperous world. For a long time in this new world, there were two people I fervently hoped to meet.

One of those was Kazuko Kojima, a resident of Kawasaki, who wrote and contributed the section to this book called 'Memories of that time'.

Mrs Kojima, whose maiden name was Fujita, was a Year 8 student, so she was one year above Yoko at school. Like Yoko, she lived in Miyajima, and travelled to Kenjo with her each day. At my younger sister's funeral, she pinned her silver Kenjo school badge to the robe that my sister had been dressed in. When Yoko was admitted to Kenjo, Japan was in the grip of an extreme materials shortage, so the only school badges available were plain ones made of aluminium. For that reason, Yoko was yearning to wear the enamel-plated silver badge that she so admired.

Knowing how Yoko had admired it, Mrs Kojima – Kazuko Fujita, as she was then – removed her own precious badge, which was irreplaceable, and pinned it to Yoko's robe with trembling fingers.

I was at an impressionable age, and for me this was an unforgettable act of compassion. Later, I moved around a lot with my job, but only the years passed; my desire to meet Mrs Kojima again remained the same.

In 1988 I was able to make contact with Mrs Kojima thanks to the NHK production *Girls in Summer Dresses*, which was broadcast throughout Japan. This allowed me to finally meet in Tokyo the woman who had made Yoko's dream come true, and to express my gratitude forty-three years after the event for her kindhearted deed.

The second person I had longed to meet was Hatsue Ueda, the woman who had cared for my dying sister in the last hours of her life at the relief centre.

Using the few clues contained in the letter that was eventually passed on to our family by Mrs Ueda's close friend, in October 1992 I finally managed to locate and visit Mrs Ueda, who was living in a rehabilitation centre on the outskirts of greater Hiroshima in Kure.

At that time, Mrs Ueda was already in her seventies, but despite her age she was a beautiful, elegant grey-haired woman with a sharp mind. I took out the old letter, which my deceased mother had so treasured, and Mrs Ueda was astonished to see her own handwriting, which had faded and changed colour over the years. Dabbing the tears from her eyes as she spoke, she told me in a clear voice about that day many years before.

The following November, I took our father, who was convalescing at home, and my wife to meet Mrs Ueda a second time, and Father was also able to thank her.

Father passed away nine months later at the age of eighty-four. I am so glad that I was able to arrange for him to meet Hatsue Ueda before he died.

It appears that my sister was promptly hospitalised and cared for at the relief centre, so the last hours of her life were peaceful.

I have also found some comfort in knowing what happened to her, thanks to Mrs Ueda.

Many of the teachers and students who were bombed and died together in Dobashi that day disappeared without a trace, and their remains have never been found. I have heard that stones collected from a beach of the Motoyasu River, beside the A-bomb Dome, were placed underneath some of the graves of Yoko's classmates.

The year of this publication in Japan, 1996, marks the fifty-first anniversary of the atomic bombings. The number of people alive today who have physically experienced the atomic bomb grows fewer with each passing year. I believe that those of us who are left behind have a duty to write and tell people about the hell on earth that we witnessed and the futility of war, so that people know the truth.

I would like to dedicate this book to all of the schoolchildren who were scattered like flower buds, believing in their country right to the end, and the teachers who died while trying to save them. I would also like to take this opportunity to respectfully pray for the repose of their souls.

Rest in peace, Yoko.

Goodbye Yoko

Yoko's diary is a small voice in the great world, one little girl's record of her life in a war zone. Like her friends, she takes it for granted that this is how she must live and behave. She never questions, or resists, or disobeys. She is a model of obedience and selfless duty.

Is this the result of her parents' insistence? Or is this Yoko's own response to the larger pressure all around her, of the war effort, her teachers, the state propaganda and the constant demands on children to work harder? It seems the answer is all of the above. Her diary reveals a little girl who is always eager to please, to do her duty, to satisfy the adult world.

Yet she also genuinely believes she is doing something worthwhile: that if she works harder she will help bring her father home, win the war, and save Japan. She believes in herself, never suspecting that her 'self' has been 'programmed' by state propaganda.

Yoko never reflects, as many Japanese adults did in private, that her efforts are in vain; that the war is lost and defeat inevitable. In this sense, she represents the triumph of the government's plan to weld the young to Japan's dismal last stand against the Americans.

Yoko is a feather in a hurricane.

PH

Acknowledgements

On the eve of the publication of this book [in Japan in 1996], I would like to express my deep gratitude to many people for their understanding, encouragement and hard work.

These include Kenzo Kamei, Masafumi Yamazaki, Kazuko Kojima, who was in the year above my sister at Kenjo, and Masako Kajiyama, who was in the same year as Yoko, and all of the students who participated in the Hiroshima Study Trip, a special course offered by Hosei University Girls' High School. Thank you for taking time out from your busy schedules to contribute to this book.

I would also like to thank the Principal of Hiroshima Minami High School, Takaaki Nakamura, and the Minami Yuho-kai Alumni Association for providing me with various materials.

I am so grateful to Hiroshi Harada, Director of the Hiroshima Peace Memorial Museum, for allowing me to take photographs of archived materials.

Special thanks must also go to Junko Kawamura of the Minami Yuho-kai Alumni Association, the writer Mitsuko Ohno, who was one of Yoko's seniors at Kenjo, and Kazuko Shishido, who was in the same year as Yoko. These people provided information about what Kenjo was like in those days.

At this late stage in my life, I am deeply moved to be finally able to publish this book thanks to the support I received from so many people.

Thank you all so much.

– Kohji Hosokawa